Emerging Party Politics in Urban Canada

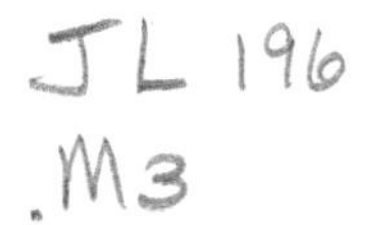

Emerging Party Politics in Urban Canada

JACK K. MASSON AND

JAMES D. ANDERSON

University of Alberta,
Edmonton, Alberta

McClelland and Stewart Limited

0-7710-0700-0

The Canadian Publishers
McClelland and Stewart Limited
25 Hollinger Road, Toronto 374

Printed and bound in Canada

Contents

Introduction

The growing awareness of urban problems in Canada has led politicians, academics, and the general public to question the effectiveness of the political process in the nation's cities. Increasingly, this critical scrutiny has focussed on the fact that political parties have not as a rule been openly involved in elections at the local level. Much of the blame for the alleged lack of responsibility and responsiveness of urban councils has been attributed to the traditional nonpartisan style of politics which has been characteristic of Canadian local government. The growing dissatisfaction with the unstructured brand of politics at this level has encouraged political parties and diverse local groups to enter civic electoral contests. As a consequence, the trend in Canada during the last decade has been towards the development of party systems in major Canadian cities.

The movement towards overt party activity has received attention in a number of books and articles written by Canadian scholars during the past decade. This book of readings incorporates selections from this body of literature, along with recent topical writings and historical material, in an attempt to provide a comprehensive treatment of the issues concerning party involvement in Canadian urban politics.

The book is designed to foster an understanding of some of the pivotal questions in the area of civic politics. A number of these key questions are raised by the diverse styles of political activity which take place in various Canadian communities. In some cities no slate or party activity is evident in civic campaigns. In others, local "nonpartisan" groups contest elections but when elected do not practise bloc voting in council policy-making. Still other cities have purely local organizations and local branches of provincial or federal parties which perform all of the functions normally associated with parties at the senior levels of government. They nominate candidates, campaign on a common platform, and when elected practise cohesive voting on council. A number of city councils, however, are characterized by a further variation. They are composed largely of aldermen who are members of provincial or federal political parties who claim to be nonpartisan in their civic role and, indeed, appear to maintain a comfortable alliance with members of other major parties.

This diversity of party-like activity has posed serious problems of conceptualization for scholars in the field of urban politics. A typology of urban elections was developed by Charles Adrian in a seminal article published in the *Western Political Quarterly* in 1959. Later, in a Canadian context, Harold Kaplan constructed a useful conceptual framework for classifying political party activity in cities. Kaplan's scheme, which is reprinted in this reader, takes the classification a step further in that he includes legislative as well as electoral activities.

Further important questions are posed by the diversity of urban political styles. What are the consequences of the various types of local politics? Are different types of political leaders elected in cities with different degrees of party activity? What values do these councillors hold? Who do they represent? To whom are they accountable? Are the policy outcomes of party-dominated councils different from those in which less partisan involvement is evident?

Recently, Canadian universities have initiated an extensive number of courses in urban studies. A noticeable void in the literature on urban Canada has resulted from the lack of explicitly political analysis. For this reason, all of the selections in this book are Canadian writings, intended to provide a deeper insight into the development of party systems in the major cities.

The book is designed primarily for three purposes. The first is to provide the student of urban politics with material which will assist him in understanding a critical topic in the urban field. Secondly, an examination of the development of party systems at the local level will give the student a perspective with which to compare the development and functions of parties at the provincial and federal level. Thirdly, the book will provide a useful supplement to the student of Canadian government and politics.

Unfortunately, many students in the field of political science seem to view the study of civic government as dull and uninteresting. We hope that the selections in this book dealing with the controversy over party involvement in civic politics will illustrate the dynamic nature of this area of political inquiry.

An extensive bibliography has been included to indicate the development of Canadian urban party politics and to suggest other relevant writings.

Jack Masson, James Anderson

1

Origins of Nonpartisan Urban Politics in Canada

Introduction

Canada's legacy of nonpartisan urban government has resulted from factors indigenous to the Canadian political environment and from the influence of the American municipal reform movement. During the latter half of the nineteenth century and the early decades of the twentieth century virtually all large American cities were governed by a strong political party system with a power base rooted in political patronage. The factors which gave rise to the urban party machine are generally thought to include the needs of the massive numbers of immigrants who flocked to urban centres; the absence of social welfare programs and civil service codes; the organizational requirements of growing cities hamstrung by institutional checks; and the existence of unregulated business corporations willing to pay for favours from civic decision-makers.

With the founding of the National Municipal League in the United States, in 1884, a proliferation of middle-class reform groups campaigned vigorously against the evils of the immigrant-based urban party machine. Their prescriptions to exclude politics from civic government included (a) the introduction of the nonpartisan ballot, (b) separation of the dates of local, and state and national elections, and (c) the commission and city-manager form of government. These reforms were designed to introduce the principles of efficiency and economy of the corporate world into local government as well as to eliminate the "irrelevant" value conflicts introduced by political parties. The clamour against the corruption of civic parties had the effect of producing a strong nonpartisan ideology which helped to insulate local parties from major party control. These devices, along with specific anti-party measures and improved social welfare measures, civil service reform and reduced immigration led to the demise of the party machine in many established cities and prevented its rise in newer communities.

Very shortly after adoption of reform proposals in the United States, they were discussed and adopted in many Canadian cities despite the fact that the party system had not been a feature of the politics of Canadian local government.

The first article in this section, written by James Anderson, discusses the historical development of the nonpartisan ideology and reform measures in Canadian local government. His article reviews the literature on Canada's local politics and sets the stage for the articles of the early writers which follow.

The selection by Samuel Morley Wickett, a professor of Political Economy at the University of Toronto, at the turn of the century, indicates why political parties had not yet obtained control of civic government. Like the American reformers, he accepts uncritically the view that party politics is an evil to be avoided in local government.

In the following selection, H. H. Gaetz, the former mayor of Red Deer, Alberta espouses the reformist view that municipal government is a matter of administration and should therefore be conducted on the principles of efficiency and economy. He reluctantly admits the importance of the electorate but then contends there is no difference between the goals of the private corporation and the municipality. W. D. Lighthall, then the mayor of Westmount, boasts of Canada's virtue in combatting the evils of political parties in his speech at the 1917 convention of the National Municipal League. Of special note is his assertion that parties were influential in early Canadian local government.

In a later work, William Munro argues that of all of the facets of Canadian politics, the government of cities has been the most susceptible to American influences. He rejects the reform view that local government is nothing more than administration and proceeds to point out that a major function of city councils is to represent value differences that exist among residents of the city.

Nonpartisan Urban Politics in Canadian Cities

J.D.ANDERSON

The anomaly in Canada of a nonpartisan local political system co-existing with partisan federal and provincial systems is often noted by students of municipal politics. It appears curious at first glance, that while Canadian local institutions are in many respects patterned after those of Britain and the United States, the tradition of partisan urban politics common to these countries has not become established in Canada. Despite increasing political party involvement in the larger Canadian urban centres during the last decade, politics in most cities remains effectively nonpartisan,[1] and even in those where parties are active, nonpartisanship is often a matter of degree.[2]

While urban party activists have not achieved much electoral success, they have, together with some influential newspapers and academics, begun to challenge many of the long-cherished ideals of local nonpartisanship. The increasing size and complexity of urban centres has also created a greater awareness that there are, indeed,

[1] See John G. Joyce, "Municipal Political Parties in Canada," Master's thesis, University of Western Ontario, 1969, p. 13; and Harold Kaplan, *Urban Political Systems: A Functional Analysis of Metro Toronto* (New York: Columbia University Press, 1967), p. 182.

[2] Harold Kaplan distinguishes three main types of urban politics according to the degree of nonpartisanship/partisanship. In his "non-factional" city, no organized groups compete in elections; in the "factional" city, slates of candidates are active in campaigns but dissolve when elected to council; in the partisan city, organized groups compete in campaigns and practice cohesive voting on council. See his *Urban Political Systems*, pp. 181-184. For an influential typology developed in an American context, see Charles Adrian, "A Typology of Non-partisan Elections," *Western Political Quarterly*, XII (June, 1959), pp. 449-458.

political issues in local government. Vocal, issue-oriented pressure groups in recent years have contributed further to the belief that all is not well with city government. The view that the nonpartisan style of politics may actually be one of the key factors responsible for the "urban crisis" has recently gained considerable acceptance, particularly among élites.

Like other political institutions, nonpartisanship is not neutral in its effects upon various groups in a given political jurisdiction.[3] Advocates of partisan local politics argue that the absence of parties from local electoral contests results in the election of councillors and councils which are different in a number of important respects from those which would have been chosen if elections were partisan. These critics maintain that in nonpartisan cities, many candidates are recruited by organized community groups whose members are almost always individuals of high status and whose occupations are often directly affected by the policies of City Hall. In addition, self-recruited candidates, motivated by a private sense of *noblesse oblige*,[4] frequently run in nonpartisan elections. Those elected to office from these two main groups are, as one would expect, quite unrepresentative of the social and class configuration of the local population. The case against nonpartisan urban politics in Canada is not unlike the argument made by Robert Lane, who claims that in American cities the absence of political parties, the chief agencies fostering political involvement of the lower class, results in the disorientation of lower-status persons, thus reducing their participation. Local politicians realize that their election does not depend upon the votes of this group and consequently become less responsive to their needs.[5]

Two other serious charges often levelled against local nonpartisanship in Canada include the claim, firstly, that the voter is prevented from voting on the basis of issues, and secondly, that there is no readily identifiable group on council to call to account if the

[3] Douglas Rae, *The Political Consequences of Electoral Laws* (New Haven: Yale University Press, 1967). See also Kaplan, *Urban Political Systems*, p. 181.

[4] James Lightbody, "The Rise of Party Politics in Canadian Local Elections," *Journal of Canadian Studies*, 6 (February, 1971), p. 43. In an American context, see Kenneth Prewitt, "Political Ambitions, Volunteerism, and Electoral Accountability," *American Political Science Review*, 64 (March, 1970), pp. 5-17.

[5] *Political Life* (New York: The Free Press, 1959), pp. 269-272.

voter is displeased with the policies of that body. Voting on the basis of the positions of the candidates on civic issues is virtually impossible, since in nonpartisan contests aspirants for office usually promise "good government," "efficient administration" and little else. In nonpartisan contests the issue-orientation, which is an element in the complex images projected by parties,[6] is largely absent. In addition, the absence of an identified majority group on nonpartisan councils allows incumbents to disclaim responsibility for unpopular decisions.[7]

Paradoxically, local nonpartisan politics may have a partisan bias.[8] Local office often serves as a "stepping stone" to senior levels of government, and municipal councils often harbour a large number of councillors who claim to be nonpartisan in their local role but at the same time hold memberships in federal or provincial political parties. It is conceivable that members of the party which is least popular in a given region of the country enjoy a greater chance at nonpartisan office than would be the case if the local system were partisan, simply because they are free from the negative impact of an unpopular party label. In the city of Edmonton, for example, the Liberals have held about half the seats on city council for the past four years, yet there have been no provincial Liberal members and only one Liberal M.P. elected from the city during this period.[9]

[6] Donald Stokes, "Voting," *International Encyclopedia of the Social Sciences* (New York: The Macmillan Company and The Free Press, 1968), p. 393.

[7] See Peter Silcox, "Everybody's Urban Crises," *The Canadian Forum* (May, 1969), p. 36; and Joyce, "Municipal Political Parties . . .," pp. 44-46.

[8] Willis Hawley, *The Partisan Bias of Nonpartisanship*, Ph.D. Dissertation, University of California, 1970.

[9] After the 1968 civic election in Edmonton, the council consisted of six Liberals, three Conservatives, one N.D.P. member, and three alderman whose senior-level party affiliations (if any) were unknown. The council elected in 1971 was made up of five Liberals, two Conservatives, two N.D.P., and three members whose affiliations were not known. See Lynne Bell, "Liberals Would Rule Parliamentary City Council," *The Edmonton Journal* (January 19, 1970), p. 25. Information on the present council was obtained from a senior Edmonton councillor interviewed in January, 1972. There are additional explanations for the large number of Liberals on the Edmonton council. It is possible that more Liberals contest the elections than members of other parties because the local level is the only one in which they can realistically hope to win. Also, it appears that a disproportionate number of the civic

Advocates of local party politics see parties as vehicles which could bridge the gap between citizen needs and demands on the one hand, and civic policy decisions on the other. Parties, in their view, would improve the policy co-ordination and innovation in urban government. Since parties are able to concentrate power, partisan government would be able to act decisively in the face of high levels of controversy and matters now the preserve of appointed officials would be dealt with by the elected representatives.[10]

The evidence supporting these alleged consequences of nonpartisanship, however, is less than conclusive. Rarely are nonpartisan cities actually compared with partisan cities although this comparison is often implicit. Indeed, in Canada such a comparative approach would be difficult because of the lack of effectively partisan cities. Nor is it easy to determine whether a particular policy orientation of a city council can be attributed to the nonpartisan nature of the city's politics or to some underlying environmental factor which might be said to determine both the policy *and* the nonpartisan political style. It is also possible that many of the consequences linked to nonpartisanship are, at least in part, the effects of other reform institutions most often found in nonpartisan cities, such as the at-large election and the city-manager plan.[11]

While these methodological problems are not in principle insoluable, to fully understand the effects of nonpartisanship it is important to know the factors involved in the origin and development of this style of politics. The purpose of this article is to examine the origin, development, and persistence in Canada of both the ideology of nonpartisanship and its institutional correlates. The significant questions that must be answered include the following: What is the origin of the attitude, so strongly held in Canada, that party politics is inappropriate in local affairs? To what degree has the development of this anti-party sentiment been indigenous to Canada and to

élite in Edmonton supports the Liberal Party. The fact that the names of the élite are relatively well-known likely enhances their electoral prospects by providing a cue to the voter, especially since the election is nonpartisan and the cue which would otherwise be provided by the party label is absent.

[10]See, for example, Lightbody, "The Rise of Party Politics . . . ."

[11]I have elaborated upon this point in Chapter IV of my Master's thesis, "Nonpartisan Civic Politics in Canada and the United States," Political Science Department, University of Alberta, 1971.

what extent does it reflect the influence of the American municipal reform movement? Why has partisan politics obtained a foothold in some cities while in others the nonpartisan tradition has persisted?

Indigenous Factors in the Development of Nonpartisan Local Politics

The fact that Canadian local government remained nonpartisan while many American cities were controlled by highly organized political party machines suggests that there were factors indigenous to Canada which explain the absence of local partisanship. The rapid urbanization which was well underway in the United States in the late nineteenth century came later in Canada. Canadian cities were small, relatively homogeneous and lacked the patronage potential available to the party machines in American cities, especially in those centres with large immigrant populations. The relationship to senior levels of government was different – the provinces exercised more control over local affairs than did the various states, and as a consequence the power base in local government in Canada was less attractive to political parties. Parties evolved in American local government partly to co-ordinate the disparate centres of local authority that existed in cities after the Civil War. In Canada, however, the practice of electing local administrative officials, the long ballot, and other Jacksonian principles were not adopted and consequently, the need for an agency such as a political party to centralize authority was not felt to the same degree.

Establishment of local government was a relatively late development in the provinces that now comprise Canada. Province-wide systems of municipalities were only established in the central provinces in the mid-nineteenth century and in the Maritimes and the West not until after confederation. Similarly, urbanization came comparatively late in Canada; in 1871, for example, Canada's urban population was only 18 per cent of the total. When the large immigrant influx began about 1896,[12] most newcomers were encouraged to settle in the rural areas. The urban centres were also quite homogeneous: in 1881, apart from French Canadians (who were confined chiefly to rural areas of Quebec and New Brunswick), 96.7

[12] Leroy Stone, *Urban Development in Canada* (Ottawa: Dominion Bureau of Statistics, 1967), pp. 4, 20.

per cent of Canada's population was of British origin. By 1891, the foreign population (British immigrants were not considered foreigners) in eight of Canada's larger cities was only 5.6 per cent – the comparable figure for fifty of the large American cities 30.8 per cent foreign-born.[13] This small scale and social homogeneity of Canadian communities suggests that there was probably little disagreement over the ends of local government and therefore insufficient political cleavage to support a system of competitive party politics. In these small communities, it was possible for the electorate[14] to have face-to-face contact with the local representatives, and partisan rivalry would have been destructive to the "politics of acquaintance"[15] that prevails in small communities.

An important strain in the ideology of nonpartisanship present in the early thinking on municipal government was the belief that the purpose of local government was to provide services. The idea that local government involves administration, not "politics," was natural in these early communities where most important functions were dealt with by senior levels of government, and where the energy of the inhabitants was directed more toward the struggle for survival in an often unfriendly natural environment than toward internal rivalries.[16]

Other historical influences contributed to the development of a local political culture inhospitable to partisan politics. Early British settlers, for example, arrived before party politics had become a dominant factor in British local government, and the Loyalist settlers who came to the colonies at the time of the American Revolution had no experience with partisan local government. Indeed, most of the Loyalists, especially those who settled in Upper Cana-

[13]Samuel Wickett, ed., *City Government in Canada* (Toronto: University of Toronto Studies: History and Econcmics, II, 1902), pp. 9-10.

[14]The restricted nature of the civic franchise in Canada served to reduce both the size and the heterogeneity of the electorate. See Wickett, *City Government in Canada*, p. 10; and Donald Rowat, *Your Local Government* (Toronto: The Macmillan Company of Canada, 1962), pp. 38-39.

[15]This phrase is used by Eugene Lee, *The Politics of Nonpartisanship* (Berkeley: University of California Press, 1960), p. 120. A detailed account of this phenomenon in small cities is found in Edward Banfield and James Wilson, *City Politics* (Cambridge: Harvard University Press, 1963), pp. 24-26.

[16]Lightbody, "The Rise of Party Politics. . . ."

da, were familiar with the New England type of local government[17] with its strong tradition of local autonomy. Any interference in local elections by national or provincial political parties would have violated this cherished independence. Before the introduction of a merit civil service, the notorious corruption associated with federal and provincial parties did little to endear them to urban residents.[18] Moreover, the tight provincial control over local governments left little opportunity for patronage in local politics, thus discouraging the entry of senior parties into the local field. A political economist from the University of Toronto stated in 1902 that there were:

> . . . certain regulations as to municipal patronage through which political spoils are in part shielded from local politicians and in part removed to the more suitable field of the province.[19]

The development of political party activity in local government in Quebec was also likely retarded by the existence of traditional local authorities such as the clergy. Consistent with this interpretation is Greenstein's view that the absence of strong traditional authorities controlling local affairs in the United States created a power vacuum which was occupied by the political party machine.[20]

Influence of the American Municipal Reform Movement

The writers on local politics in Canada are almost unanimous in attributing the nonpartisan tradition in Canada to the influence of the American municipal reform movement. Though these observers place too little emphasis upon the indigenous Canadian factors discussed above, it is nevertheless quite evident that the anti-party

[17] Kenneth Crawford, *Canadian Municipal Government* (Toronto: University of Toronto Press, 1954), p. 22.

[18] See, for example, W. L. Morton, *The Kingdom of Canada*, second edition (Toronto: McClelland and Stewart Limited, 1969), p. 423. Also, Norman Ward, *The Canadian House of Commons: Representation*, second edition (Toronto: University of Toronto Press, 1963).

[19] Wickett, *City Government in Canada*, pp. 10-11.

[20] Fred Greenstein, "The Changing Pattern of Urban Party Politics," *Annals of the American Academy of Political and Social Sciences*, 353 (May, 1964), pp. 1-13. It is worth noting that the appearance of effective political party control of Montreal city council coincided with the beginning of Quebec's "quiet revolution" which marked a distinct shift from the traditional parish-oriented values.

ideology of the reform era played a significant role in keeping party politics out of Canadian cities. William Bennet Munro's famous comment is no exaggeration:

> Of all branches of government in Canada, the government of cities has proved the most susceptible to American influence.[21]

The municipal reform movement which had such a profound impact on Canadian urban politics, began in the United States in response to the corruption associated with the urban political party machine. As early as the 1870's a number of "good government" leagues, led chiefly by academics and small businessmen, began to appear in American cities. Many of these groups joined together in 1884 to form the National Municipal League which became the leading organization of the reform movement. Though the rhetoric of these middle-class reform groups attacked the political immorality of the party bosses, much of their opposition probably resulted from the loss of their formerly unchallenged role as civic leaders, and they saw in the elimination of party politics a means by which their values could again dominate civic affairs. The nonpartisan ideology that these reformers propounded, along with the structural changes they proposed, had remarkable success in insulating American city politics from partisan influences.[22]

By the time Canadian cities reached the size and complexity sufficient to make them attractive to political parties, the reform ideology and the accompanying structural innovations imported from the United States had become firmly established, and provided an effective barrier to the entry of parties. Cities of the western and southern regions of the United States followed a similar pattern of political development. They became important centres relatively late in American history, after the municipal reform movement had created a climate inhospitable to the old partisan political style, and like Canadian cities, most of them have remained nonpartisan.[23]

[21] *American Influences on Canadian Government* (Toronto: The Macmillan Company of Canada, 1929), p. 99.

[22] Oliver Williams and Charles Adrian, "The Insulation of Local Politics Under the Non-Partisan Ballot," *American Political Science Review*, 53 (December, 1959), pp. 1052-1063.

[23] Raymond Wolfinger and John Field, "Political Ethos and the Structure of Local Government," *American Political Science Review*, 60 (September, 1966), p. 326.

Both the attitudinal and institutional dimensions of nonpartisanship in Canadian urban politics can be traced to the American municipal reform movement. A number of ideas about civic government, which together form a virtual ideology of nonpartisanship in Canada, are largely American in origin. These include the belief that urban government is a matter of administration or "business" to be "managed" according to the business principles of efficiency and economy; that there are no "political" issues in civic government; that political parties introduce irrelevant issues into local administration and that they are inherently corrupt. Many institutional devices designed to eliminate parties in American cities were, ironically, adopted in Canada despite the fact that there were no local parties to eliminate in this country. The nonpartisan ballot was irrelevant in Canada where local elections, like national and provincial elections, had always been formally nonpartisan in this sense. But the other two elements of the "reform package," the city-manager plan and the at-large election, did gain wide acceptance in Canada.

The nonpartisan tradition, as Donald Rowat suggests, was imported into Canada ". . . after the local nonpartisan movement in the United States had become strong."[24] This anti-party ideology was firmly held by influential figures in Canada by the first years of the present century. In 1912, for example, the Municipal Auditor of Ontario stated that party politics in local government could be kept out ". . . so long as citizens are alert to protect the best interests of the city against the intrigues of ambitious politicians."[25] Remarks made by W. D. Lighthall, then the mayor of Westmount and honorary secretary of the Union of Canadian Municipalities, suggests how pervasive the anti-party feeling had become. In a speech to a group of American reformers in 1917, he boasted that in Canada:

> . . . the elimination of [municipal] party politics is a universally accepted sentiment. It is supported by all influential newspapers and is strongly in favor with all classes of people.[26]

[24] Donald Rowat, *Your Local Government*, pp. 34-36.

[25] J. W. Sharpe, "Government by Commission," *The Municipal World*, 22 (December, 1912), p. 274.

[26] W. D. Lighthall, "The Elimination of Political Parties in Canadian Cities," *National Municipal Review*, 6 (March, 1917), p. 208.

An important agency involved in the export of nonpartisanship to Canada was the influential American reform organization, the National Municipal League. In 1913 it held its twenty-first National Conference for Good City Government in Toronto, the only conference it ever held outside the United States. At this time also, the League was answering inquiries from Canadians and sending its literature to them.[27] The pivotal role played by the League was highlighted by remarks made by the ubiquitous Mr. Lighthall in 1918:

> In that intercommunication which is of late years constantly taking place between the municipalities of the United States and those of Canada, largely through the National Municipal League and the Union of Canadian Municipalities . . . Our cities usually look to yours for experience.[28]

During this period, the consensus among Canadians familiar with municipal affairs seemed to be that the United States was the source from which Canada should get ideas to improve her municipal system. As Munro points out, not only was the nomenclature of Canadian local government more akin to that of the United States than to that of Britain, but Canadian municipalities were also more like the American municipal system in form and practice.[29] This tendency to look to the south is illustrated by the report of the Commission on Municipal Institutions set up by Ontario which reported, in 1888, that it had concentrated its research on American cities because:

> . . . the circumstances of the people in that country more nearly resemble our own in rural and urban districts, and we may reasonably conclude that whatever works satisfactorily amongst them is not wholly unsuited to us.[30]

[27] Frank Stewart, *A Half Century of Municipal Reform: The History of the National Municipal League* (Berkeley and Los Angeles: University of California Press, 1950), p. 164.

[28] W. D. Lighthall, "War Time Experiences of Canadian Cities," *National Municipal Review*, 7 (January, 1918), p. 19.

[29] Munro, *American Influences*, Chapter III.

[30] Cited in H. L. Brittain, *Local Government in Canada* (Toronto: Ryerson Press, 1951), p. 13.

Nonpartisan sentiment became particularly strong in the Canadian West where almost a million Americans from the Progressive stronghold of the American plains settled, chiefly during the period between 1898 and 1914.[31] These settlers brought with them the anti-party attitudes characteristic of the Progressive movement of the United States, and this influence undoubtedly contributed to the nonpartisan style of politics in cities that appeared later in the West.

A militant farmers' organization of American origin, the Patrons of Industry, gained popularity in the West (and in Ontario) after the 1880's. The Patrons stressed the familiar reform notion that government is a matter of business and that political parties bring corruption and inefficiency to government. A declaration in the 1896 edition of the *Patron's Advocate* called for an end to "out of date party methods and procedures" and advocated "the application of business methods to public matters."[32]

Another farmers' organization of American origin, the Non-Partisan League, originated in North Dakota and spread to the prairie provinces in the second decade of this century, where it carried out a vigorous attack on the evils of party politics. It was publishing two weekly newspapers in Saskatchewan by 1917, and in that same year the Alberta publication of the League, *The Alberta Non-Partisan* claimed a circulation of 7,000.[33] The philosophy of the League emphasized "a repudiation of party politics"[34] and was aimed at establishing so-called business government which would deal with public issues on their merits rather than on the basis of party considerations. During this same period, the *Grain Grower's Guide* also carried out a consistent attack on party politics.[35] Although this opposition to parties came largely from the farm population, the nonpartisan tradition present in cities like Edmonton and Calgary today likely reflects to some degree the thinking of

[31] Richard Hofstadter, *The Age of Reform* (New York: Alfred A. Knopf, 1955), p. 53.

[32] Cited in M. S. Donnelly, *The Government of Manitoba* (Toronto: University of Toronto Press, 1963), p. 104.

[33] Vol. I, No. 25, (October 26, 1917).

[34] Morton, *Kingdom of Canada*, p. 423.

[35] C. B. MacPherson, *Democracy in Alberta* (Toronto: University of Toronto Press, 1953), p. 40.

formerly rural people who have migrated to these centres in recent decades.

Shortly after the turn of the century American reformers, who were finding through painful experience that it was difficult to dislodge the urban party machine without changing the conditions which gave rise to it, began to concentrate their efforts upon changing the structure of city government. The "reform package" that was advocated consisted of the nonpartisan ballot, the city-manager plan (or council-manager plan) and the at-large election. These structural innovations, designed to replace the evil of party politics with the honest, efficient administration by experts was incorporated into the "Model City Charter" of the National Municipal League and received sustained promotion in the League's influential publication, *The National Municipal Review.* Not only was promotional information on these nonpartisan devices spread to Canada by the publicity efforts of the League, but the International City Manager's Association also carried on "... an energetic propaganda for the further extension of this [manager] plan in Canada."[36]

The city-manager plan became popular in Canada after its origin in the United States in 1910 and can still be found in numerous Canadian cities today. The at-large form of election, designed to undermine the ward-based political organizations, was also adopted in a number of Canadian cities.[37] Other reform devices, such as the nonpartisan ballot, and the separation of the dates of local and senior-level elections, were irrelevant in Canada where party label had not been in use and where the dates of local elections rarely coincided with provincial or national contests.

The importation of the reform structures into Canadian urban government reflected an acceptance of the nonpartisan ideology which was explicitly linked with these new forms. In 1909, for example, H. H. Gaetz, the former mayor of Red Deer, in a speech

[36] Munro, *American Influences*, pp. 127-128.

[37] The traditional election of Mayor by the councillors from among their own ranks was replaced by the practice of popular election to this office, thus ending the situation in which the fortunes of mayor and council were bound together. The change to electing councillors at-large also created a situation in which each candidate was competing against all the others. Both practices hindered the development of partisan local elections since it provided a disincentive to candidates who might otherwise have campaigned on a group basis.

to the Union of Alberta Municipalities denounced the "baneful influence of party politics" in municipal affairs and suggested that every member of the Union "secure a copy of the Municipal Program ... of the National Municipal League." He then quoted approvingly from remarks by President Elliot of Harvard University: "'Municipal Government is pure business and nothing else – absolutely nothing else ... and the ward basis has no intelligent foundation.'"[38]

Not only is the view of civic government as administration still strongly held, but it is often directly linked to the question of non partisanship. In a study of all alderman and mayors in Edmonton between 1964 and 1967, for example, Donald Blake found that most of them were opposed to parties at the local level ... "'cities provide mainly services' was a representative response."[39] In a more recent nation-wide survey of elected municipal officials, Joyce found that his respondents agreed almost unanimously that the service function was the main task of city government.[40] Given the uncanny instinct for political survival exhibited by urban politicians in Canada, it is likely that their support of nonpartisanship is a fairly accurate reflection of the opinion of the electorate of most cities. The practice of split-ticket voting in recent Toronto civic elections where parties have openly entered the contest indicates the tenacity of the belief in voting for the man rather than the party.[41] Until recently, the nonpartisan ideology has not received support in the major city newspapers[42] and parties themselves have seldom openly contested civic elections, fearing a voter backlash. Aldermen affiliated with provincial or national parties have traditionally preferred to

[38] H. H. Gaetz, "Municipal Legislation," *The Western Municipal News*, 4 (March, 1909), pp. 1078-1081.

[39] "Role Perceptions of Local Decision-Makers," Master's thesis, University of Alberta, 1967, p. 77.

[40] Joyce, "Municipal Political Parties ...," p. 24.

[41] See, for example, Peter Silcox, "Postscript ... City Council Results," in *Parties to Change* (Toronto: Bureau of Municipal Research, 1971), p. 56.

[42] For example, an editorial in the October 20, 1945, *Edmonton Journal* stated that "... for years the *Edmonton Journal* has protested and opposed any appearance of a federal or provincial party in Municipal elections." More recently the same newspaper has come out in favour of local party politics. See the editions of September 3, 1968, and September 11, 1971.

downplay their party ties in their municipal role. This persistent nonpartisan tradition in Canadian urban politics refutes a recent observation by Charles Adrian that nonpartisanship "seems to be a uniquely American ideology."[43]

Emerging Party Politics

A form of partisanship appeared in urban politics in the 1920's and 1930's, particularly in western Canada. The socialist and labour groups of the period began to run candidates in civic elections where they were confronted by "nonpartisan" slates composed largely of Liberal and Conservative businessmen who organized to "save the city from socialism." Ironically, the labour-oriented assault on City Hall was itself a response to the traditional domination of civic politics by the business élite. The reaction to the Winnipeg General Strike of 1919, and to the "Red Scare" in the United States in that same year helped awaken the traditional civic élites to the need to oppose labour and socialist groups at the civic level.[44] A labour coalition succeeded in controlling Regina's city council for several years in the late 1930's[45] but western cities have usually been dominated by establishment slates. This has been true in the case of the Civic Election Committee in Winnipeg, and the Non-Partisan Association in Vancouver, for example. In Edmonton, the majority of aldermen elected have usually been supported by business-oriented slate-making organizations.[46] Yet, despite the success of these slates in the electoral arena, they often vote on an individual basis in council. Their orientation seems to be essentially negative – designed to keep the socialists out of City Hall, but lacking any well-formulated political program of their own. These slates, however, perform many party-like functions in city politics

[43]Charles Adrian, "Nonpartisanship," *International Encyclopedia of the Social Sciences* (New York: Macmillan, and Free Press), p. 202.

[44]D. C. Masters, *The Winnipeg General Strike* (Toronto: University of Toronto Press, 1950); also, see his, *Coming of Age* (Montreal: Canadian Broadcasting Corporation, 1967), p. 15.

[45]W. J. C. Cherwinski, *Organized Labour in Saskatchewan: The TLC Years, 1905-1945*, Ph.D. Dissertation (History) University of Alberta, 1971, p. 262.

[46]G. M. Betts, "The Edmonton Aldermanic Election of 1962," Master's thesis, University of Alberta, 1963.

and are becoming more like traditional parties as they face an increasing challenge from reform-oriented political parties.

The success of Mayor Drapeau's Civic Party in Montreal in 1960 provided an important impetus to the development of partisan politics in other large cities. The Civic Party showed that urban politics can run openly on a partisan basis, and that this can be done by a local partisan organization free from ties with federal or provincial parties. The fact that the most striking example of urban party politics arose in Montreal suggests that the reform ideals that have become imbedded in the political culture of English-speaking Canada has probably not had the same impact in Quebec because of the linguistic and cultural barriers.

The much-publicized entry of the Liberal and New Democratic Parties into the 1969 Toronto civic election indicates that the non partisan tradition in major English-speaking cities may be giving way. Observers have pointed out, however, that the parties were not entirely successful in the Toronto election of 1969 – electing only five official Liberal and N.D.P. candidates to the twenty-three positions on council.[47] It is important to note, however, that this was the first overtly partisan contest in Toronto and in addition to the many barriers to entry[48] present in the local political milieu, the internal divisions within both N.D.P. and Liberal parties thwarted a concerted partisan effort. The pressure exerted by upwardly-mobile (and in particular the more ideological) party activists however, is likely to tip the scales against old-guard party members who maintain a vested interest in nonpartisan civic politics.

Despite the decisive defeat of the New Democratic Party in the October, 1971, civic election in Winnipeg, the results can be interpreted as a continuation of the trend to a more partisan form of urban politics. While the New Democrats won only seven of the fifty seats, the Independent Citizens' Election Committee (ICEC), which took thirty-seven seats, operated in almost every sense as a

[47]E. P. Fowler and M. D. Goldrick, "The Toronto Election of 1969: Patterns of Partisan and Nonpartisan Balloting," Paper presented at the annual meeting of the Canadian Political Science Association, Winnipeg, Manitoba, June 4, 1970, p. 36.

[48]Stephen Clarkson, "Barrier to Entry of Parties into Toronto's Civic Politics: Towards a Theory of Party Penetration," *Canadian Journal of Political Science*, 4 (June, 1971), pp. 206-223.

political party. The ICEC campaigned as a group on the basis of a program which it formulated at a two-day policy convention, and the day after the election the campaign chairman stated that its members would also hold caucus meetings.[49] The example of the Independent Citizens' Election Committee suggests that an increasingly partisan form of urban politics will evolve as municipal branches of senior-level parties make a concerted effort at civic office. The threat these parties (especially the N.D.P.) pose to the traditional civic élites forces the latter to form, what is in effect, an opposing political party. The fact that only five independents were elected from the list of sixty-seven who ran for office in the October, 1971, Winnipeg election suggests that the unaffiliated, nonpartisan alderman may soon be a rarity in the larger cities. The results of the 1970 civic election in Vancouver, in which independents received less than five per cent of the vote, also tends to support such a view.[50]

The emerging pattern of party politics in Canadian cities is due largely to the fact that it is in the interest of some influential political élites to structure it that way – the majority of the urban population is either indifferent or opposed.[51] If the élites continue to attempt to structure their struggle for civic office along partisan lines, however, the electorate will have little choice but to vote for party candidates. In the long run, the political parties active at the provincial and federal levels are likely to dominate civic politics as well. In Britain and the United States, the senior parties have replaced local organizations which lack the membership, finances and organizational resources of senior-level parties. Local parties are often too dependent upon the personal qualities of an individual leader and may fail to survive beyond the end of his career.

[49] *Winnipeg Free Press*, (October 7, 1971), p. 18.

[50] Fern Miller, "Politics in Vancouver: Developing a Model of Party-System Change and Stabilization," unpublished paper, Political Science Department, Yale University, December, 1971.

[51] There is, unfortunately, very little survey data on the attitudes of Canadians toward local government. In a survey of a random sample of the Edmonton electorate, however, Robert Gilsdorf found that 73.3 per cent of his respondents approved of the way their (non-partisan) city was governed. See Jack Masson and Robert Gilsdorf, "Studies of the Urban Environment: A Political Science Perspective"; and R. G. McIntosh and I. E. Housego, eds., *Urbanization and Urban Life in Alberta* (Edmonton: Alberta Human Resources Research Council, 1970), p. 39.

As the majority of Canadians become concentrated in a few urban centres, the social diversity of these cities will approach that of the province and nation. Social problems will increasingly become urban problems. Élites will view civic politics as an important arena in which to implement their social philosophies and to realize their political ambitions. The necessity for political parties to appear relevant in a largely urban Canadian society suggests that their involvement in urban politics is likely to increase.

City Governments in Canada

S.M.WICKETT

Precedent in the United States,[1] . . . has influenced Canadian civic organization in many important respects. For this reason, and because New World influences also prevail in Canada, certain features of city government in the United States may be used as a standard of comparison. In the simplicity of its detailed organization, however, urban government in Canada approximates rather to the English than to the American type.

Perhaps the most striking contrast between municipal organization in Canada and in the United States is found in the one being in a state of free development, while the other is conditioned by the requirements of a system. In Canada the municipal constitution is changing from Parliament to Parliament, from session to session, unfolding new powers here, dropping others there, according as requirements dictate or experience advises. In the United States the springing up of large towns and the rapid growth of great metropolitan centres have necessitated their being housed in administrative structures for which the lines were suggested, as Mr. Bryce and others point out,[2] by the already existing state governments. That the process of adaptation demanded many alterations was to be expected, for city and state are so differently conditioned, both from

From *City Government in Canada* (Toronto, University of Toronto Studies, History and Economics, Vol. II, No. 1, University Library, 1909), pp. 3, 5, 7-12, 14-15, 21-23.

[1] *Cf.* First Report of the Ontario Municipal Commission of 1888, p. 22.

[2] Bryce, as cited, Vol. 1, Ch. I; and Goodnow, *Municipal Problems*, pp. 16, 21, where the author speaks of a too strict adherence in American municipal legislation to doctrinaire teachings.

the standpoint of party politics and from that of general administration, that an organization which has been eminently successful for the state may not be at all adapted to the smaller unit.[3] In Canada, on the other hand, the municipal organization is in the main the outcome of gradual development and forms therefore a reliable reflection of local growth. The series of municipal amendments passed from session to session of the provincial legislatures, mostly on the initiative of the local councils, bears this out. . . .

A second important factor in Canadian municipal growth is the homogeneity of the population – setting aside the French element, which forms practically a distinct group in a single province.[4] In this respect again, the contrast with the United States is marked. In 1891, in every 100 of the population 96.7 were of British and 1.2 of United States birth. This leaves but the small percentage of 2.1 to be credited to all other nationalities. Or, taking Ottawa, Montreal and six out of the seven provincial capitals (that of Prince Edward Island not being specially referred to in the census report), we find that in 100 of the mean population of these cities only 5.6 were foreign born; or, excluding settlers from the United States, merely 3.21. This makes a striking comparison with the latter country. In every 100 of the mean population of the fifty largest cities of the United States 30.77 are foreign born; in the rest of the country 11.29. The homogeneity of Canada's population certainly simplifies the problem of city government. Montreal and Ottawa alone among the cities appear to be somewhat trammelled in their municipal activity by racial and concomitant religious influences. Of Montreal's population considerably over one-half is French Canadian, of Ottawa's one-third.

[3] *Cf.* Eaton, *The Government of Municipalities*, pp. 63, *et seq.*

[4] The census of 1891 returns 1,404,974, or 29 per cent of the Dominion's population as of French descent. As these figures are based on the *de jure* system of enumeration, under which people are enumerated according to their permanent domicile, they probably include many thousands, probably many tens of thousands, of French Canadians working in New England factories. Of these 1,186,346, or 85 per cent of those enumerated, are ascribed to the province of Quebec. Quebec (City), since the withdrawal of the British regulars some years ago, is now almost altogether French Canadian, although at present one or two of its aldermen are British Canadians. Of the 91,605 French Canadians (6.5 per cent of the whole) returned for Nova Scotia and New Brunswick very few appear in the larger towns or cities.

A restricted municipal franchise is a third feature of urban government in Canada. In Nova Scotia and St. John's (Nfld.) the qualification for municipal voters resembles that required in England – namely, twelve months' residence within the municipality and payment of poor and city rates, for which the voters must not be in arrears. . . .

But while homogeneity of population and a restricted franchise have undoubtedly favoured municipal government in Canada, they do not altogether explain its unusually placid course. An influence perhaps even more potent is the comparative non-interference of political parties. Here again is presented a striking contrast to conditions in the United States. Generally speaking, public opinion in Canada has been thus far opposed to the direct introduction of party politics into municipal matters. Partisan influences are, it is true, never wholly absent; in a few places they are decidedly active, though this is fortunately the exception. The explanation of this exemption from political interference will be found mainly in the smallness of many of the cities, the homogeneity of the population and the predominance of local interests and influences.[5] To this should be added the conservatism of the civic franchise, and certain regulations as to municipal patronage, through which political spoils are in part shielded from local politicians and in part removed to the more suitable field of the province.

Municipal offices are filled, not by popular election, but by mayor and council. Moreover, as a rule, the appointments are not for a specified term, but in practice are permanent during good behaviour.

On the whole, though perfection is not written across the face of city organization or administration in the Dominion, the basis of city government in Canada must be said to have been "well and truly laid." The conservatism of the urban franchise; the homogene-

[5]In contrast to conditions in many parts of the American Union, the dates for provincial and federal elections are fixed independently of the municipal elections, with which they may be said practically never to conflict. This is the more likely since city elections, with but few exceptions, are held between the months of December and April. The absence of party, or some other organization to fill its place has, however, left the bringing forward of municipal candidates largely to interested parties, self-help and chance. This condition of affairs has told heavily on the representative character of the aldermen. Happily, however, we have some valiant workers in the municipal field.

ity of the city population, which the future will probably not affect to the same extent as in the United States; the general policy with regard to municipal patronage and the consequent absence in large measure of party politics in city elections; and, finally, the efficacy of "conservative innovation" and gradual growth and expansion of municipal legislation – these are features whose importance cannot be lost sight of. The conditions for good city government seem, therefore, propitious. Certainly the phrase, "the one conspicuous failure," which Mr. Bryce applies to the government of cities in the United States, will not be held applicable to city government in Canada. But it will not do for Canadians to boast. They are not yet out of the wood. Foreign elements are coming more into evidence in some of the cities, and there are many problems yet to be settled concerning the relations of province and city, and important matters more directly affecting municipal organization still to be disposed of. Of these the corporation question in its various aspects is one of overshadowing importance.

Municipal Legislation

H.H.GAETZ

Our Municipal Councils know nothing of party politics and its baneful influence, dividing men on lines having no bearing upon the interests of the Municipality; neither bossism nor the vested rights of Public Service Corporations have yet thrown about us their demoralizing influences. Nor are we hampered by the traditions of a past. We are free to build our institutions on the bed rock of common sense and honesty of purpose, making our own precedents if we do not find established ones that suit our purpose.

Not only in America but in England as well it is being realized that the elective council combining the functions of legislation and administration is a very weak and ineffective instrument, responsible almost wholly for lavish expenditure coupled with inefficient service where these exist.

More especially in this new land of ours, where every active man's energy is taxed to the utmost in his own concerns, there is no leisured class of men whose time can be devoted to public affairs. For this reason, as our Municipalities grow, it will become increasingly difficult to secure the services of desirable men on our Councils, if these Councils continue to divide the responsibilities of administration among committees of their own body. On the other hand with the executive duties vested in competent salaried officials and the duties of Councillors confined to those of Legislation and direction our best men would consider it an honor and a pleasure to

Paper presented to the Union of Alberta Municipalities Convention by the ex-mayor of Red Deer, Alberta. Published in *The Western Municipal News*, Vol. IV (March, 1909), pp. 1078-1081.

serve the Municipality as they serve upon the directing boards of important business organizations.

Nor are these men, however competent they may be to handle a business for which they have been carefully trained through many years, fitted by training and experience for the important undertakings which are suddenly placed in their hands upon election to office. It is no particular discredit to them if they fail, as they usually do, to handle their departments with wisdom and discretion.

The elective council is a weak instrument of administration also because there is possible with it no continuity of purpose which alone can make large undertakings successful. Moreover under such a system responsibility is too easily shifted; there is no head to cut off when things go wrong. Somebody else is always to blame. Imagine for a moment if you can a great business organization whose administration would be carried out by a board elected by the stockholders and divided into Committees as our Councils. What would happen to it? The thing is too absurd to dwell upon.

Then why should we persist in applying a method so palpably absurd to the highly important business under consideration?

The Governmental organization of Municipalities has two functions to perform, the one to give expression to the popular will and the other to execute its edicts. A perfectly clear line of distinction should be made between these two functions and the organization should be clearly divided into legislative and executive bodies and the duties of each specifically defined. The legislative body should come frequently in touch with the popular will through the agency of frequent elections, while the executive body must needs possess a more permanent tenure of office to insure efficiency and continuity of administration. Speaking broadly the duties of a council should, besides the regulation of its own organization and procedure, be to enact local ordinances; to issue franchises (subject to referendum) to control public property; to levy taxes; to borrow money; to apportion expenditures; to appoint and remove chief administrative officials and to determine certain broad lines of policy.

I would like to quote some passages from an address of President Elliot of Harvard University, delivered before the Economic Club of Boston, on January 11th, 1907:

Municipal Government is pure business and nothing else – abso-

> lutely nothing else. To the performance of business functions in an intelligent and honest manner, the notion of representation by districts of population has no sensible application. There is no representation of that sort needed and the ward basis has no intelligent foundation.

Further on he said, after speaking eloquently of the need of experts to handle Municipal affairs:

> I can only say that all the successful business of this country is conducted by small groups of men in all our great corporations, generally men of a good deal of experience in the business. It is one of the most preposterous things in our City Government that the personnel is so frequently changed. The Aldermen and Councilmen are no sooner come than they are gone and we are generally glad of it. It is an absurd way of conducting a great business. It is not Government we are after in the City. It is not controlling people. It is not deciding on great policies of business development or of tariff even. It is getting the business of the people done straight. Let us simply emulate the example of the successful Corporations of our Country. They get their business done well as a rule.

I quote these words particularly to add the weight of a great name to the contention which I now advance *viz.* that as the work of the Municipal Organization is business "pure business" we should endeavor to organize our administrations on the pattern of the successful business corporations whose form has been perfected in the hot fires of necessity fanned by the tempestuous winds of competition.

I think I may be permitted to disgress for a moment however to administer one more kick to the retreating figure of Ward representation. I have yet to hear of any authority of moment, whether theoretical or practical who has anything good to say of this foolish, unbusinesslike and uneconomical method of representation which President Elliot scores so severely, except perhaps to some extent in some cities of Metropolitan proportions, and I hope that our promised Municipal Corporations Act will at least do something to assist the expulsion of this undesirable feature of Municipal Government.

To return to the question of Municipal business. It is contended by some that the two organizations, the municipal and the business, have little or nothing in common, that the latter is conducted for the purpose of procuring a profit on the investment and operation, while the former is not conducted with this end in view I contend however that there is no difference; that whether dividends to shareholders or the greatest material advantages to the ratepayers is the object sought after the principle is the same and that the methods which have proved successful in accomplishing the one aim will prove as effective in accomplishing the other.

To apply the principles laid down here to the framework of Municipal Government we would have in the first place a body of voters having an interest in the Municipality or in other words a property qualification as at present.

I would strongly recommend that every member of this Union who wishes to pursue this subject, (and I presume that includes all) should secure a copy of the Municipal Program from the Secretary of the National Municipal League, an American organization that is doing much to reform Municipal methods on this Continent. The Municipal Program is the result on (*sic*) some years of labor by a committee of expert Municipal men and outlines a model bill which while not providing for such radical methods as I have here advocated; is full of suggestion and assistance along the lines that we are now so deeply interested in. In drafting an Act for Alberta our Legislature could not do better than follow it closely in determining the nature and form of the powers which should be vested in Alberta Municipalities.

The Elimination of Political Parties in Canadian Cities

W.D.LIGHTHALL

The reason why I am called to address you to-day is that I come from a land whose people, in a true and profound sense, are part of your people, bone of your bone, sinew of your sinew, speech of your speech, spirit of your spirit; who, pervaded with the atmosphere of ideals and circumstances of this continent are, in the broad meaning, as American as you; and who, in their origin and growth, are in substance an overflow of the population of these United States. Before the revolution, New England people had begun to found what are now our provinces, and after the revolution the great basis of our population was laid by the loyalist refugees from every state, and by perhaps an equal number of others than loyalists who followed the rich opportunities of our territory. Even to-day one of the best and largest sources of our immigration is the stream of hundreds of thousands of American farmers who have taken up our western lands. I might go further, into a historical digression, and show that the British Empire, itself, had its origin among those same men of vision who gave birth to the idea of the united colonies. Both of those ideas began together before the revolution. It was our common American ancestors who dreamed them – the greatest political visions in the world.

It is, therefore, not surprising that our municipal institutions are essentially American – essentially on the same patterns as your own, with differences rather of experimentation and local accident than of structure. One of those local accidents is a very fortunate one – the elimination of political parties from our municipal politics. In this,

From *National Municipal Review*, Vol. VI, (March, 1917), pp. 207-209.

perhaps, we may contribute something to your information, just as we constantly learn innumerable things from your municipal experience. Between Canada and the United States there is a great contrast in this matter.

We see with astonishment such things as Republican or Democratic control in the governments of your cities, tickets of candidates representing Republicans or Democrats, the evils of general party rancour introduced into local affairs, and too often we hear of the spoils system playing an only too important part in the result. In Canada, on the other hand, a party ticket in municipal affairs is unknown. A man's party opinions may gain him some votes, but merely in the same way as his association with the masons or the independent order of moose have made him some incidental friends. The mere suggestion that party strife entered into the matter would arouse strong opposition among the voters and in most cases the candidate would be fain to publicly repudiate the suggestion in order not to lose his election. In short the introduction of party issues and shibboleths nearly everywhere in Canada is regarded as a dangerous and outlawed principle.

Just how this has come to be is somewhat difficult to determine. Certainly it was not so in our early municipal elections, eighty years ago, which were of a highly spicy and unladylike variety. Now, on the contrary, it is a fair statement that the elimination of party politics is a universally accepted sentiment. It is supported by all influential newspapers and strongly in favor with all classes of people. Its strength lies in the fact that it has become an attitude of mind, firmly fixed by *habit.* It certainly produces very beneficial results – a greater freedom and insistence upon the personal fitness of the candidate, a much reduced difficulty in finding really suitable candidates, and a sense that a candidate, once elected, is tied to no group of men, at least on party grounds. But the chief advantage is that it severs the municipal policy from all sorts of state and federal considerations. It thus enables a municipality to come before its legislature standing on the merits of its demands.

Now, from the modest acquaintance I have with American municipal affairs, based mainly on a long association with the National Municipal League and other American municipal bodies, and also partly on a constant reading of the newspapers, I know that many of your municipal experts sometimes envy us this advantage, and wonder how it can be introduced in the United States, and added to your long list of important municipal triumphs.

Let me make only two remarks on that question: – *First*, that, whatever be the method, the *object* should be *to attain a habit of public mind* against the continuance of the party system. In Canada it rests upon a habit of public mind acquired during the past half century, and favored no doubt by the fact that our party methods have never attained such completeness of system as your own. They have never come down to such refinements as your party tickets. The *second point* is that, whether the process be long or short, simple or difficult, – and there is no doubt it will be difficult – I have absolute confidence in the American people, in their ability to achieve any idea. The elimination of party politics will come to you as it has to us, sometime – and within a reasonable time. The struggle for it is not a hopeless one, and ought to be pursued systematically with optimism, and having as its set purpose the *gradual creation of the necessary habit of public thought.*

As the representative here of the Union of Canadian Municipalities, I bring you the profound congratulations and the absolute sympathy of the Canadian people in all your splendid work.

City Government in Canada

W.B.MUNRO

Of all branches of government in Canada, the government of cities has proved the most susceptible to American influence. In the form and spirit of their government Canadian cities have been steadily moving away from English standards and veering toward the organization and methods of municipalities in the United States. This is not surprising. The contacts between the cities of the two countries are much closer than are those between the rural areas. Canadians who know most about the United States, and who visit it most frequently, are mainly from the cities. The so-termed "agencies of American penetration," concerning which there is so much protest in Canada from time to time, are most active in the cities. American newspapers, magazines, and moving pictures naturally have a greater influence in the urban than in the rural portions of Canada. . . .

In the United States during the past half-century there has been maintained the world's chief laboratory for experimentation in municipal government. England, for nearly a hundred years, has made no substantial change in her municipal organization. Liverpool, Leeds, Manchester, and Bradford are governed today under a Municipal Corporations Act that has not been appreciably altered since 1835. But in the United States no city is governed as it was even thirty years ago. The changes both in form and spirit of American city government have been far-reaching during the past three decades, and they have attracted much attention in Canada

From *American Influences on Canadian Government* (Toronto: The Macmillan Company of Canada, 1929), pp. 99-105, 109-110, 119-120, 122-133, 140-143. Reprinted by permission of The Macmillan Company of Canada Limited.

because they have seemed to suggest ways of meeting problems that are fundamentally alike in the two countries.

The New World differs from the Old in many things, but in nothing more conspicuously than in the problems of urban growth and administration. Canadian cities have very little in common with the boroughs of Great Britain – whether in their physical characteristics, their rapidity of growth, their relations with the surrounding country, or their civic resources. The organic kinship of Toronto is with Buffalo, not with Sheffield. Winnipeg and Vancouver more nearly resemble Minneapolis and Seattle than Edinburgh and Manchester in their needs, problems, individuality, and point of view. The rapid growth and astounding prosperity of cities along the northern fringe of the United States (such as Cleveland, Buffalo, Detroit, and Chicago) have afforded Canadians an impressive object-lesson. It is not surprising that they should be interested in what these exuberant communities are doing and should at times accord them the tribute of imitation. . . .

The principle of checks and balances, for example, which is altogether at variance with English traditions of local government, but is peculiarly American, has been gradually working its way into the Canadian system until it is now definitely established. Its tacit acceptance in Canadian cities has given a new cast to the entire municipal organization. There is a division of power between the city council (which is vested with legislative authority) and various independent or semi-independent boards (sometimes including a Board of Control) with functions which are chiefly administrative. This divorce of administrative functions from direct dependence upon the legislative organ of local government, to the extent that it has been accomplished in Canada, is the complete negation of English theory and practice. . . . From the American federal government the bifurcation of authority worked its way into all the states and ultimately into the government of cities as well. Then, from the bottom up, it began its invasion of Canada. . . .

Canadian cities did not adopt the elective mayoralty on its merits; it is merely a transplantation from the United States where it owed its inception to the frontier democracy of Andrew Jackson and his philosophy of "keeping government close to the people. . . ."

The Board of Control idea originated in New York City about

half a century ago. It was chiefly inspired by a desire to take away from the municipal council its freedom of action in matters of expenditure. Aldermen of the American metropolis, elected by wards, were found to have no sense of economy. Checks and balances gave way to cheques and deficits. They ran the city into extravagance and debt. So the power to propose expenditures was taken away from these aldermen and given to a Board of Estimate and Apportionment, as it was called, made up of the mayor and certain other members, all of them owing their places to popular election. The New York Board now consists of eight members, including the mayor. All are elected directly by the people. The Board prepares business for the aldermen (of whom there are sixty five elected by districts); it prepares the estimates, awards contracts, and grants franchises; but its actions in some cases may be set aside by a three-fourths vote of the larger body. . . .

English cities are among the best-governed in the world and largely because the entire responsibility for every branch of municipal administration is concentrated in a single body – the City Council. The Council has surrendered none of its powers or functions into the hands of boards or commissions or committees which it does not directly control. Canadian cities, by contrast, have been abandoning this principle of centralized responsibility, replacing it by the American system of disintegrated municipal authority even though that plan has become thoroughly discredited in the land of its birth. American cities are today bending their efforts to the task of getting away from the system of independent boards, and bringing all municipal authority to a single focus. The popularity of the city manager plan is due in no small measure to the fact that it provides a definite centre of accountability. . . .

Complaint is made, both in the United States and in Canada, that citizens of the right sort are reluctant to serve on City Councils, and we are sometimes told that this betokens a lack of civic patriotism on their part; but the trouble goes deeper. There is plenty of civic patriotism on both sides of the line when it is given a fair chance to exemplify itself. To afford this chance, public office must be clothed with power and with the opportunity to render constructive service. Meanwhile, in American cities, the board system of administration has broken down and is being everywhere replaced by a scheme of local government which makes the head of each department directly responsible to the mayor or the city manager as the case may be. One does not give a hostage to fortune in predicting that the board system will eventually break down in Canadian cities also, for the functions of a modern municipality are too extensive, too complicated, and too important for efficient administration by a series of independent and semi-independent commissions. There must be some articulating force. . . .

One might, indeed, venture to suggest the wisdom of letting American cities demonstrate the success or failure of their municipal experiments before Canadian cities proceed to copy their methods; but this course has rarely been pursued. Fifteen years ago, for example, when the "commission plan" of city government was having a transient popularity in the United States, some Canadian cities made haste to provide themselves with this new and wholly untried scheme of local administration. The old framework of mayor and council was replaced by a single board of five elective commissioners. These five commissioners constituted virtually the entire government of the city, being mayor and city council and heads of departments all combined in one. Each commissioner under this plan, served as the head of a department (or rather as the head of a group of departments) while the five commissioners, sitting together, passed the by-laws, voted the estimates, awarded contracts, and made all appointments. The commission plan of city government embodied an extreme reaction against the principle of divided powers, and as such it was widely heralded as affording a simple remedy for the various shortcomings of municipal administration in the United States.

But the plan soon proved to be unsound in theory and unsatisfactory in its workings. A board of five men, however chosen, is too small to be adequately representative of all the substantial interests and points of view in a large community. On the other hand it is too large to function satisfactorily as a channel of executive responsibility. The defects of the plan are organic, not merely incidental. They became so apparent within a few years that one American city after another has abandoned the commission plan. Of the three hundred or more American cities, large and small, which adopted the commission plan during the years 1900-1915, more than two thirds have now discarded it. St. John, N.B., is the only Canadian city which maintains this form of government at the present time and there the original plan has been considerably modified.

To-day it is the city manager plan (or council-manager plan) of city government that is having its wave of popularity throughout the United States. This newest form of municipal organization has been installed in nearly four hundred American cities, including such large centres as Cleveland, Cincinnati, Rochester, Indianapolis, and Kansas City. It likewise has made its way into Canada, although not yet on an extensive scale. The manager form of government has been established, however, in two Ontario cities (Chatham and Niagara Falls) and in fifteen other municipalities scattered from Manitoba to New Brunswick. An energetic propaganda for the further extension of this plan in Canada is now being carried on – in part through the agency of the International City Managers' Association, and the chances of its further spread are considerable.

The essential features of this council-manager government can be explained in a few words. A City Council is elected in the usual way, either by wards or from the city at large. This council decides all matters of municipal policy, votes the estimates and adopts the by-laws. But it does not carry out these policies when determined upon, or make any appointments, or control the various commissioners or heads of departments. Instead it is required to appoint an official known as the City Manager to whom it must hand over all these administrative functions. In other words, the government of the city is approximated to that of a business corporation. The voters, as stockholders of the municipality, elect a board of directors, the City Council. These directors appoint a general manager who conducts the business subject to their general supervision and control. . . .

For every branch of local government (except the schools which are continued under a Board of Education) the City Manager is directly responsible, and he holds office only so long as he retains the confidence of a majority in the Council. In other words, he is the prime minister of the municipal parliament.

This plan of government undoubtedly has merits. It is simple, intelligible, and potentially efficient. It eliminates friction among the departments and brings responsibility to a common centre. It conforms to the practice of corporate business. Indeed, it is grounded on the idea that what we call city government is business, not government. It assumes that efficient municipal administration is not largely a matter of passing by-laws and voting the estimates, but of paving streets, awarding contracts, supplying water and light, protecting life and property, and appointing officials. The advocates of the manager plan tell us that inasmuch as the city has business to do it should have a business organization to do it – which is plausible enough, although by no means altogether convincing.

It is not convincing because there are at least two reasons why the business analogy cannot be applied to city government without large reservations. In the first place the board of directors in a business organization is a unit, both in interests and in point of view – which the City Council is not and cannot be. For the prime purpose of a City Council is to give representation to a variety of sections, interests, and points of view among the people. It follows that the direction and control of municipal policy will inevitably be made subservient to the interplay of these sectional and political influences, which means that there is bound to be controversy, and friction, and some working at cross purposes within the Council's ranks. For of such is the Kingdom of Democracy. It is not possible to give the city a strictly business organization unless the representative principle is largely abandoned. So long as a City Council is representative of the people it will reflect diversity of opinions, for ratepayers do not all think alike when they think at all.

There is a second reason. Those who share in the management of an incorporated business have some definite financial interest in it and their voting power is proportioned to that interest. Business policy is controlled by the pocket nerve. But those who control the destinies of an incorporated municipality have in many cases no direct financial stake. In large urban communities, many of the electors are not assessed as ratepayers. They own no taxable property. They have no personal concern with the municipal tax rate, or think they have none. To most of those who are not themselves ratepayers the announcement of an increase in the city's tax rate is about as devoid of personal interest as are the statistics of average rainfall and temperature. It is futile to press the business analogy in city government so long as those who control the spending are not the ones who directly provide the revenue. It is true, of course, that every elector is a taxpayer in an indirect way – for whoever pays rent, pays taxes, and whoever buys merchandise pays taxes; but that is not the point. Many of the electors are not *conscious* ratepayers, and it is the consciousness of taxpaying that counts. . . .

In the last analysis the political orientation of the Canadian West is a wide variant from that of Whitehall and Westminster. The atmosphere of public administration in Regina, Saskatoon, and Edmonton is far more nearly like that of Duluth, Denver, and Tacoma. Geography and race, throughout the whole North American West, on both sides of the international boundary, will constrain the people to look at their similar problems from much the same point of view. That is a commonplace, or ought to be; but even the commonplaces of political determinism are not to be despised. It is in the order of nature that American usages will continue to be shown hospitality by Canadians both West and East especially when they arrive incognito. . . .

In the practice of free government, the enforcement of law, the administration of justice, and the encouragement of municipal home rule, there is no country that excels England, the Mother of Parliaments. The governmental traditions of that sceptered isle are Canada's heritage: they ought not to be lightly cast aside. Canadian government, whether federal, provincial, or municipal, will be no better and no worse than Canadians choose to make it. There is no such thing as "manifest destiny" so far as political standards are concerned. Every country, every city, has as good or as bad government as it deserves; for with the unalienable right to govern themselves must go the right of a people to misgovern as well. Sound traditions are therefore more vital than constitutions and laws, however wisely framed, for it is the spirit of a government that determines its worth.

2

Parties and Politics in Canadian Cities

Introduction

This section includes articles examining increasing party activity in Canada's two largest cities. During the past decade there has been a definite trend toward overt party activity in our large urban centres. The Civic Party of Jean Drapeau has effectively controlled the Montreal city council for the past ten years and 1969 saw the organized bid for power in the city of Toronto by two major parties, the N.D.P. and Liberals. In Vancouver in 1970 the N.D.P. contested the election openly under the party banner opposing the "nonpartisan" group headed by Mayor Tom Campbell. In October, 1971, the N.D.P. made a concerted bid for power in the Winnipeg civic election and was defeated by a "nonpartisan" civic party. The indications are that not only are many citizens more willing to accept party politics as a means to solve the growing urban problems, but also that party activists see in the growing public concern with urban ills increasing opportunities for their political ambitions.

In the first article, Edmund Fowler and Michael Goldrick consider the implications that the introduction of partisan electoral politics has for both the political élite and voters' behaviour in Toronto. More information is provided on the recent Toronto election in the exchange between J. L. Granatstein and Stephen Clarkson. Their debate revolves around a recurring theme in the controversy on urban politics – whether strictly local parties or adjuncts of major provincial and federal parties are able to do a more effective job of governing the city.

This section concludes with two articles on civic politics in

Montreal, the only large city in Canada where the policy-making of council is tightly controlled by an overtly partisan organization. Albert Tremblay discusses the organization of the dominant Civic Party and the actions of its dynamic leader, Jean Drapeau. Margaret Daly, a feature writer for the *Toronto Star*, offers a sympathetic treatment of the opposition reform party in Montreal, the Front d'Action Politique (FRAP).

Patterns of Partisan and Nonpartisan Balloting

E.P.FOWLER & M.D.GOLDRICK

The Entrance of Parties

National political parties invaded Toronto's municipal elections in 1969. Not only was it the first intervention of parties on anything like this scale in Canadian cities, but it also ran counter to a North American trend away from partisan urban politics that has prevailed since the beginning of the century.

The purpose of this paper is to consider the effect of the shift from nonpartisan to partisan electoral politics on voting behaviour in the City of Toronto and to offer some explanation for differences in its modest impact on different sectors of the political community. We begin by considering why and how national parties came to commit themselves or abstain from participation in the election, since this helps to explain the limited impact that they had. Anticipating the argument somewhat, it is clear that the Liberal and New Democratic party élites decided in favour of involvement in response not to public clamour for party politics but primarily in response to partisan and personal considerations. In doing so, they committed the common error of vastly over-estimating the mass public's political knowledge, perception, and concern for ends which the élites thought partisan municipal politics would achieve.

Unquestionably, a series of what might be termed environmental factors created a hospitable climate for partisanship. One of these is a critical size that cities such as Toronto appear to reach when devices like parties become desirable. A large population, hetero-

From *Parties to Change: The Introduction of Political Parties in the 1969 Toronto Municipal Election*, Bureau of Municipal Research, Toronto, 1971, pp. 34-45. (Slightly revised by the authors.) Reprinted by permission.

geneity, specialization, complexity of issues require institutionalized means to aggregate interests and to provide voters and politicians with a kind of political shorthand with which to sort out issues and appropriate responses. A second factor was the growing dismay with the council system in Toronto, which seemed to conspire against any coherent form of political leadership. Each member of the City Council operated in a sense as one of twenty-three parties, one for each elected position. One is reminded of the Grand Inquisitor's song in The Gondoliers:

> And party leaders you might meet
> In twos and threes in every street
> Maintaining with no little heat
> Their various opinions.
> . . . In short, whoever you may be
> To this conclusion you'll agree:
> When everyone is somebody,
> Then no one's anybody.

Ad hoc coalitions formed, usually on an issue to issue basis. And nowhere was the fragmented nature of the council more evident than in elections, when citizens were asked to vote for individual candidates who were effectively free from accountability.

This situation had an impact on concerned élites, at least, for whom the introduction of political parties was one of several needed structural changes. A leading voice in this chorus was the Toronto press, which campaigned vigorously for parties in editorial columns from about 1966 on. The attention paid to this issue by the press was extremely important in creating an atmosphere conducive to partisan politics. It is interesting to note, however, that Stephen Clarkson, a mayoralty candidate, has since charged that newspapers were indifferent to the existence of parties during the actual campaign. But as the communication medium of the political élite, newspapers defined and articulated the issue, making it common currency among those few who stopped at the editorial page *en route* to marriages, births, and deaths.

Stephen Clarkson, "Barriers to Entry of Parties into Toronto's Civic Politics: Towards a Theory of Party Penetration," *Canadian Journal of Political Science*, Vol. 4 (June, 1971), pp. 206-223.

The formation of Civac, a so-called "nonpartisan party," in 1966, gave form and substance to the question of civic parties and through its birth pangs provided material for newspaper discussion of the entire issue. Civac also served as an important test-bed, providing an opportunity for national party activists, especially those of the Liberals, to try on party politics for size. Involvement with Civac broadened the experience of many and widened the circle of those who were interested in a new form of municipal politics.

A final environmental factor that sharpened the relevance of partisanship was the popularization and growing discussion of the "cities crisis." The impact of race, violence, and poverty on cities in the United States focused attention on the condition of urban life, and in a local context, a series of issues – expressway construction, airport location, redevelopment, governmental reform, pollution – and new styles of political activity by citizen groups, appeared to stimulate in many for the first time a consciousness of the city.

These environmental factors helped to create a climate amenable to change, but they did not stir up a groundswell of popular support for party involvement, though they did provide reasons and some justification for party politics at local level to a handful of political sophisticates within parties and outside them. Decisive influence, however, was exerted by party activists. The responses of these influentials to the issues of partisanship were governed on the one hand by the effect of entry on their personal aspirations in party and political life and on the other by their assessments of the benefits or electoral costs of entry in terms of their particular parties.

The importance of both factors can be explained by the unique character of parties. Parties share with other systems of social organization a number of structural characteristics. Two are important for present purposes. First, as opposed to conventional bureaucratic forms of organization, they are voluntary. There are no overt economic incentives and few sanctions to induce participation. Maintenance of membership depends on a continual flow of benefits from party to members which are traded for party support. Such benefits may be ideological or personally instrumental, the latter including the achievement of political ambitions.[2] Through

[2] See, S. J. Eldersveld, *Political Parties* (Chicago: Rand McNally, 1965), chapter 1.

party affiliation, members attempt to maximize the ideological and personal gratifications they receive. The realization of their personal ambitions is functional for the party in the sense that the higher the level of satisfaction achieved within it, the greater the level of support for the pursuit of party goals. If incentives are inadequate, members may look elsewhere for the gratifications they anticipated from party work.

It is as true of party work as of the military that every soldier carries a field marshal's baton in his knapsack. In the Toronto case, there are unrealized ambitions among party activists, especially those of the Liberal and New Democratic parties, workers on the make, faithful supporters who had "done their mile" for other aspirants, and newcomers who wanted to get out on the hustings. For the Liberals the overwhelming electoral success of 1968 left in its wake confidence, vigour and a cadre of workers whose ambitions were whetted rather than slaked by federal election victories. Similarly, the N.D.P., which had unabashedly flirted with municipal politics since 1964, recorded some electoral success in 1968 and felt that its provincial position was improving in the Metropolitan Toronto area. It too was optimistic and well endowed with party hopefuls. Significantly, and in sharp contrast, the Progressive Conservatives were in veritable disarray. Wiped out federally, the party in Toronto was tightly controlled by an entrenched organization which was itself dominated by a rurally oriented and less than secure provincial government. The spark that seemed to inhabit the other parties was not evident in the Conservative camp. Thus the Liberal and New Democratic parties seemed in a mood to dare to innovate and had members who were itching to move from constituency backrooms to council front office. It was these who made the running for party intervention, testing the *status quo* and pushing for new opportunities to absorb their ambition. The entry of these parties into municipal politics provided an appropriate outlet while the relative paucity of similarly motivated adherents in the Progressive Conservative party contributed to its decision to abstain from overt participation in the election.

A second relevant characteristic of parties is referred to by Michels as their omnibus tendency.[3] Parties generally are "greedy,

[3] S. J. Eldersveld, *ibid.*, p. 5.

for members." They are continually engaged in recruitment, for to the extent that they are able to broaden the base of their committed support, their chances of achieving the primary party goal of electoral success are enhanced. However, linked to this is a further imperative of party organization which has already been alluded to; this is the informal and indistinct nature of the role of members. In contrast to bureaucratic organizations, positions are poorly defined, tasks indefinite, and movement between positions largely unsystematic. Thus, if the base of the party is expanded, opportunities for members to derive gratifications from their association must be found if their support is to be retained.

The Liberal and New Democratic parties were motivated by these kinds of considerations. Both could see solid advantages in full-blown participation though in neither case, of course, was this the unanimous judgment of their members. Municipal activity for both parties offered a means to animate and involve party adherents and at the same time to broaden the base of their popular support. For the Liberal party, the latter point was something of a departure. While involvement in local politics had been an accustomed part of party rhetoric since the early nineteen sixties, it received its first real stimulus from Trudeau and subsequently was sanctified by the writings of the National President, Senator Richard Stanbury.

If municipal politics could enhance the mass party or populist image of the Liberals, it could do this and more for the N.D.P., particularly in the Toronto area. After some coolness toward municipal involvement by the party, the Toronto Labour Council came down solidly in favour of it during 1968. This was the result of dwindling influence by organized labour during the nineteen sixties in the government of Toronto. In addition, it was felt by some in the labour movement that municipal politics and its attendant opportunities for community work and social animation offered an appropriate means to involve the more than 120,000 trade unionists in Metropolitan Toronto in their unions and party.

For both parties, municipal involvement promised to employ under-utilized human resources and mobilize new support. The Progressive Conservatives, on the other hand, were not in such an expansionist mood. Some members who advocated partisan involvement certainly regarded it as a means to rejuvenate the party's flagging fortunes but they were not persuasive.

A third party incentive to involvement was the conventional wisdom holding that the Toronto City Council and, in fact, most municipal governments in Metropolitan Toronto were dominated by undeclared Tories.[4] While this provided an added incentive to the Liberals and N.D.P., it was obviously a factor which militated against any adventure by the Progressive Conservatives.

Looking at the other side of the ledger, there were real obstacles to party intervention which, on the part of the Tories, prevailed. Foremost of these was the financial one. From the Progressive Conservative side, it was argued that since the conservative minded candidates already were achieving considerable electoral success, their only demand on the party could be for campaign funds which it could ill afford. As the momentum for involvement by the Liberal party picked up, tacit support from its highest reaches gave some assurance but no promise of financial assistance for a campaign. But concern in this respect was important in both the Liberal and New Democratic parties.

Primary opposition in all three parties came from incumbent politicians. The greatest influence of this kind was present in the Progressive Conservative party, but all incumbents were reluctant to tamper with what for them was a successful arrangement.

Two other factors militating against party involvement were particularly important. Again for the Tories, the party organization dominated by the provincial government could see few advantages and many potential problems in dealing with a Conservative City Council, let alone an antagonistic one. This was less a concern for the other parties, the provincial and federal levels of which were more indifferent at least initially, than anything else. However, the eventual endorsement of municipal participation by the provincial leaders of the Liberals and New Democrats prior to the election probably indicated a belief that the local parties could help build a provincial challenge.

Finally, the question of adequate leadership was important in the parties' decisions. The national Liberal and Progressive Conservative parties traditionally have placed great emphasis on the image projected by their leadership. The fact that the Progressive

[4] See: Bureau of Municipal Research, *The Metro Politician – A Profile* (Toronto, June 1963).

Conservatives were unable to produce a mayoralty candidate who could project a strong, purposeful public image was a major reason for their rejection of intervention. The Liberals, on the other hand, courted "public figures" from every sector of the community finally settling on a relatively unknown candidate who was unable to establish himself adequately in the short time available. Whether consistency with a national convention of this kind is essential in a municipal setting such as Toronto is a matter of conjecture. But the electoral success of the N.D.P., (a party which tends to be stronger in its organization than in the image of its leader, in federal politics), lends some support to the idea that it is not a matter of conjecture. Though the incumbent Mayor of Toronto, William Dennison, was a member of the N.D.P., he refused to campaign as a party candidate. After a good deal of rancorous debate, the Party decided not to contest the mayoralty with an official candidate but, as we make clear below, it still was able to project a distinctive party image to a significant degree.

The outcome of this interplay of forces was that the Tories passed while the Liberals and N.D.P. plunged. The point that should be emphasized here is that while what we have called environmental conditions created an atmosphere more congenial to partisan electoral politics than ever before, the decision to contest the 1969 election was made by political party activists acting on the basis of personal and party considerations. The decision was not made in response to popular demand, though on that score, the political élites may well have mistaken their own voices, amplified by the press, for those of the people.

Voter Receptivity

In the preceding pages, we have indicated some of the considerations affecting politicians and political parties entering the Toronto municipal election of 1969. All that was prior to the campaign and the election. The crushing fact is, of course, that the City's voters could not seem to have cared less about the introduction of parties into the election. There are some who dispute this, arguing that party candidates received half the votes which were cast. On the other hand, they also fielded half of the candidates. The best evidence we have comes from some data we collected ourselves.

When the votes were counted on election day, students from York University were present in 33 polls selected at random in each of 11 wards throughout Toronto, recording the votes of every seventh ballot as they were counted. For a small proportion of the City's polls, therefore, we were able to ascertain the number of people who voted a straight Liberal Council ticket and the number of people who voted for both N.D.P. candidates for aldermen[5] – neither alternative, of course, was possible in all the wards. Of 33 polls, only 13 could be characterized as having a glimmer of partisan spirit; these partisan polls are compared with each other, and with the total sample below.

At the level of the individual ballot, out of the 544 people who made up our sample, only 35 voted for two or more Liberals and 22 voted for two New Democrats. Out of the 35 Liberals only 7 voted the full ticket (two aldermen and mayor). Since it was impossible to vote a ticket in many wards (the full Liberal ticket was only possible in five of the eleven wards, for instance), we obtained a slightly different measure of ticket voting[6] by adding up the votes for the most popular Liberal in each poll where it was possible to vote the full ticket, and dividing it by the number voting the Liberal ticket. A parallel computation gave us a figure for the N.D.P. The results are shown in Table 1.

Granted, it is easier to vote for two than three persons, so some of the N.D.P. voting may have happened by chance. But it also

Table 1. Ticket Voting in The Toronto Municipal Elections

Party	Sum of votes of most popular party candidates*	Number of persons voting a full ticket	Per Cent voting full ticket
Liberal	201	7	3.5
N.D.P.	69	22	31.9

* In polls where it was possible to vote full ticket.

[5] Here we acknowledge with thanks the help of our colleague, Professor F. F. Schindeler who suggested this technique to us.

[6] Each voter could vote for two aldermanic, one mayoral and two school trustee candidates. Because the turnout for trustee elections was so light we had to ignore them; "ticket" voting was construed as voting for two or more candidates of the same party.

takes considerably more knowledge to vote for two aldermen of the same party than for the mayor and an alderman: there was only one case where a voter chose both Liberal aldermen and voted against the Liberal candidate for Mayor, Stephen Clarkson, while there were 27 cases where Clarkson and one alderman were picked out.

Table 1 indicates two things. First, there was practically no ticket voting in Toronto's elections in 1969, both because no chance was afforded the electorate to practice it and because they chose not to structure their vote in that way. Second, where such voting did occur, it was among the N.D.P. voters, who had no party mayoralty candidate, as such, to head the ticket.

This evidence leads one to ask, did it make any difference that parties were introduced into the Toronto elections? Our thesis is that yes, it did, but we contend that the introduction of parties was more the result of a significant change at the élite level than the cause of a shift of habits of voting. We are suggesting that parties were inevitable in Toronto elections no matter what the projections of success were for individual parties or for their difficulties in cracking the system. This means that politicians craved organized competition in urban politics, *whether or not they felt the electorate was ready or interested in it.* But in addition, Toronto presents an illuminating case of variations in the relationships between élites and non-élites, as represented by the difference between N.D.P. and Liberal ticket voting.

There are two links in our chain of reasoning. The first link was the personal ambitions and perceptions of party activists, which we discussed above. The second link concerned voting behaviour.

The fundamental point to be remembered (and it often is not) is that while the party label usually serves as a cue to the unsophisticated voter, in general, the distance between the ideological world of political élites and that of the average voter should be measured in light years.[7] In an extremely perceptive article, Converse has challenged the notion that the election of a particular party, or a change in government, indicates that in even the vaguest sense some voters shifted, for rational reasons, from one side of the partisan

[7]This hyperbole is borrowed from V. O. Key's, *Southern Politics.*

fence to the other.[8] The voter most likely to switch his vote has practically no knowledge of the political system, let alone the particular issues of an election. Generally, the more partisan the voter, the more likely he is to be informed on the issues of an election. That is, his unwillingness to be swayed grows as his information grows. This is something of a paradox, of course, given the extent to which the ostensible purpose of many campaign debates is to persuade the doubters. The people who are "doubters" seldom expose themselves to the debate, while the people who are informed tend to be irreconcilably committed.

Once all this has been said, it may still be argued that when two or three parties are consistently contesting one election after another, many voters (often well over 50 per cent) form stable and well defined images of those parties and their positions *vis-à-vis* the voter himself.[9] In fact, the party is the single most significant cue for the average American voter, although it has been questioned whether this is in fact the case for the Canadian voter in national elections.[10] But there are differences in adherence to party. For the less[11] sophisticated, the party is generally the *only* political cue they have for voting, hence, not a very strong one. Party loyalty grows with political sophistication, as the better informed voter finds more and more reference groups and issues to reinforce his party choice. Only among the most sophisticated is there a slight reduction in party loyalty.

The lesson to be drawn is that the broad mass of voters depends on the simple cue of parties to help them structure their vote, but the most consistent partisans are reinforced in their preference by perceptions of the candidates, of issues in the election, or of links between their group affiliations and party policy. When parties are absent, the voter tends to rely on familiarity of the name of the candidate or his ethnic group or neighbourhood; but many floaters flounder. The results of nonpartisan elections in U.S. cities have been well documented:

[8] P. E. Converse, "The Nature of Belief Systems in Mass Publics," in D. E. Apter, *Ideology and Discontent* (New York: Free Press, 1964).

[9] *Ibid.*

[10] Regenstreif, *The Diefenbaker Era* (Toronto: Longmans, 1965).

[11] The least sophisticated seldom vote and are not really aware of parties.

- the participation rate of the lower classes is cut lower than the rate of the middle and upper classes who are more sophisticated and who don't rely on only the party to "cue" their vote.[12]
- for those who do vote, other reference points are used, such as one's religion or ethnic background, one's neighbourhood, or the familiarity of the name.[13]
- disorganized non-partisan politics makes it more difficult to legislate a program of politics, and in general for city government to innovate.[14]

Our point is that in moving from a nonpartisan to a partisan system, parties have to overcome the inertia of some of these voting habits, but that some parties can do it more easily than others. In effect, donning the party label means that élites are changing their relationship with the voter, to make it easier for him to choose among alternative candidates. But the N.D.P. was able to make contact with the voter – they were able to overcome the inertia of the past – far more easily than the Liberals. Why?

We can only answer this question after looking at profiles of the polls which tended to vote N.D.P. and Liberal tickets, i.e., at least one voter in the poll voted for two or more candidates from the same party.

The group of Liberal polls are obviously better-heeled; four of the eight polls are in the silk stocking wards running north along Yonge Street. It should be remembered that the incidence of ticket voting is still very slight among Liberals, relative to the N.D.P. The group of N.D.P. polls are the other end of the socio-economic scale. While residents of these polls are more likely to own their houses, their dwelling units are worth less and their socio-economic status is considerably lower than both the city-wide average and the Liberal polls.

[12] E. C. Banfield and J. O. Wilson, *City Politics* (Cambridge: Harvard University Press, 1963), pp. 159-160.

[13] G. Pomper, "Ethnic and Group Voting in Nonpartisan Municipal Elections," *Public Opinion Quarterly*, Vol. 30 (Spring, 1966).

[14] R. Lineberry and E. Fowler, "Reformism and Public Policy in American Cities," *American Political Science Review*, LXI, No. 3, (September 1967), pp. 701-716.

Table 2. N.D.P./Liberal Polls Compared with the Whole City

	Liberal polls tending to vote ticket N=8	N.D.P. polls tending to vote ticket N=5	Entire Sample N=32
% owner occupied dwelling units	28	62	45
% protestants	70	50	57
occupation*	3.75	2.00	2.78
assessed value of individual units**	$3956	$2928	$3496

* The figures were derived for occupation by coding: working class – 1; lower-middle class – 2; middle class – 3; middle class to upper-middle class – 4; upper-middle class to upper class – 5. All of the occupation values for the residents of a ward were totalled and divided by the number of people in the ward in order to obtain an occupation value.

** This data obtained from Toronto Assessment Polls.

Normally the Liberal party attracts a large and heterogeneous electoral following. The data show that in the 1969 Toronto elections only a very thin upper stratum of Liberals responded to the partisan trumpet. These people are likely to be among the political élite themselves; at the very least they are upper-middle class and politically quite sophisticated. The Liberal Party cue just did not penetrate below this upper fringe.[15] The N.D.P. normally appeals to a specific, labour-oriented electorate, and 1969 in Toronto was no exception. Even though voters in the lower-middle class polls are much less likely to be politically sophisticated, they responded quite respectably to the N.D.P. label. In short, the Liberals did not attract their usual following, while the N.D.P. did. Why?

Our discussion of the internal structure and the electoral tactics of the two parties helps explain this difference. The Liberal Party is oriented toward its leaders and does not have as distinctive a

[15] With roughly 120 polls to each ward, we have 2.5 per cent of all polls in our sample; and with every seventh voter in these polls, .357 per cent = 1/280 of the potential electorate. Seven in the sample voted the straight Liberal ticket, which implies 7 times 280 = 2000 Liberal élite in Toronto who might have voted a party ticket. (Their turnout was obviously high.)

personality as the N.D.P. In fact, it was Trudeau as much as the Liberals who won in Toronto in 1968. The N.D.P., on the other hand, no matter what level of government, has a separate labour image which attracts a faithful core of voters. It is also more of a mass party, so that an adherent is more likely to feel strongly about his party than a Liberal is. The New Democratic party supporter relies less on strong reinforcement of party loyalty by leaders, issues and other reference groups than the Liberal supporter. A potential Liberal supporter who has voted regularly in previous municipal elections needed to reorient his image of city leaders, issues and groups to reinforce his loyalty to Toronto Liberals: after all, this kind of reinforcement is necessary for regular Liberal voting at the national level. The unsophisticated Liberal voter just did not have the information or the political energy to perform this feat in one election. The N.D.P. voter had no such task.

Regardless of the motives of individual politicians, the nature of Toronto politics is changing, and partisan elections reflect that change. For instance, many issues are becoming political that once were not: pollution, expressways and rapid transit, housing, tenant-landlord relations, ward boundaries, school location, waterfront development. The Spadina expressway controversy has demonstrated that building an urban superhighway is no longer an administrative decision; contrary to the credo of American "good government" reformers, there *is* a liberal and conservative way to pave a street. This does not mean that in a non-partisan system people do not fight about such issues. But Toronto has reached a size at which larger numbers of people are interested in more issues, and multiple issues tend to be grouped.

This grouping process – as well as the multiplication of issues in a developing political system – has not been adequately studied. One clue to its operation comes from the political psychologists who argue that man needs to structure his political perceptions because if he has too many disconnected opinions of anything, he becomes confused and unable to act.[16] It's obviously the political élite who are more likely to have too many political perceptions, for the masses operate on so few. Thus, the need to structure a city's

[16] L. Festinger, *A Theory of Cognitive Dissonance*, (Evanston: Rowe Peterson, 1957).

multiple problems and organize them into a platform of action will come from the politically involved first, those who group themselves one way or another, though parties are the most usual form. These groupings then serve a second purpose for the political élite: when they compete for political office the mass of voters are not asked to "categorize" each candidate separately, but to use his organized affiliation to cue their votes. As we have seen in Toronto, the process of organizing and reaching the voter varies from party to party. The important point is that few studies exist which treat practice as anything but a *fait accompli*, initiating action, rather than the struggling product of a maturing political system.

Politicians and political scientists both tend to think of parties as dynamic forces which influence the course of political systems. There is nothing wrong with this, of course, except that parties' behaviour itself is susceptible to a wide range of influences such as the ones described above – all their energy is not self-generated. To a greater extent than many other social groupings, parties are sensitive to extra-organizational influences and the vagaries of their members' motivations. Furthermore, parties soon acquire a keen instinct for survival and this constitutes a potent influence on their behaviour. Our major point in this paper is that parties are intermediate organizations between the masses and institutions of government, and are both cause and effect of changes in the political system.[17] We have seen how the Liberal party paid the price of not recognizing this clearly enough.

Research, in addition, has usually compared nonpartisan with partisan cities: it has not considered why one city might move from one system to another. With Toronto, we have seen several things about the dynamics of this change process. First, the élites decide to alter the rules of the game; since they are the ones who play the game, the rules are most important to them.[18] Once having structured themselves according to parties, the élites then try to filter this restructuring down to the electorate. It reaches them not in any explicit sense, but merely as semi-conscious cues for the average citizen's casual half-interest in politics.

[17] Eldersveld, *op. cit.*

[18] Robert Dahl, *Who Governs?* (Yale University Press, 1961).

Secondly, élites differ in their relations with the electorate, and their success in introducing changes in the system may vary according to their different relations. The Liberals were much less successful in reaching the electorate than the N.D.P.

Finally, parties seem to be reflectors of changes in the issues faced by a political system as much as they are innovators. Perhaps we shall be able to observe this phenomenon again as more non-partisan cities approach Toronto's size and complexity.

The New City Politics

J.L.GRANATSTEIN

The introduction of party politics into the Toronto elections last month met with a crushing rejection from the voters. The Liberal mayoralty candidate drew a bare twenty per cent of the vote and accomplished nothing beyond ensuring the defeat of the only alternative to three more years of Bulldozer Bill Dennison. Two Liberal aldermen were elected, one of whom was an old City Hall warhorse with probably the worst voting record on Council. The N.D.P. did somewhat better, electing three aldermen, all of whom promise to be several cuts above the norm.

Is party politics now dead at the municipal levels? Certainly the parties all pledged undying efforts after the results came in, but surely we have time for a second look. Why should the voters of Toronto or any other city troop out to the polls to vote for the Ottawa-based parties? Why, in fact, should they participate in the national parties' attempts to facilitate their task of political organization? God knows that Ottawa has paid scant attention to the problems of the cities.

Still, something might be gained by the formation of independent local parties, responsible only to the municipal voters. A local party system would end the destructive self-aggrandizement practised by aldermen and mayors by forcing them to conform to a party platform. It would in addition finally force the voters to take sides between those whose concept of development is limited only to concrete, and those who still persist in seeing cities as a place where people can live.

From *The Canadian Forum*, January, 1970, p. 226. Reprinted by permission.

Toronto particularly is fortunate to have in its inner core a hard, talented group of urban thinkers who see the need for community control of redevelopment and who oppose the mindless sprawl of high-rise apartments and expressways. These people are the basis for a municipal political party founded on a philosophy of radical conservatism. To conserve: to oppose the advocates of *progress* whose prime interest is, as always, to make a buck. Radical: to give power to the people, to the community. This is what the new city politics should be about.

Already there is one alderman on the Toronto City Council who embodies this approach. This is John Sewell, a young lawyer, who was elected with hand-lettered signs (prepared by his mother!) on a surge of support from people in a ward threatened by urban "development." If Sewell can function effectively in Council, he will give a boost to those who are already working to organize an effective urban coalition on a radically conservative basis. The election three years hence will be their opportunity. It may also be the very last chance to save Toronto.

The New City Politics — A Reply to Old Cliches

STEPHEN CLARKSON

One of the few disheartening aspects of my otherwise exhilarating campaign as Liberal candidate for the mayoralty of Toronto was the hostility expressed by some citizens towards party politics. Reading Jack Granatstein's editorial on "The New City Politics" in the January *Forum* is surprisingly like hearing a badly scratched record of the misconceptions about party politics which haunted Toronto's municipal election. It is not just "J.G.'s" summary interpretation of the results which are inadequate. He fails to see the entry of parties into municipal politics in the historical perspective of the transformation under way in the large Canadian cities. As the public becomes aware of the dimensions of its urban crisis, pressure has been growing to make City Hall responsible to community demands and powerful enough to deal with the city's own problems.

A glance at the platforms of the three Toronto municipal parties would have shown J.G. how they expressed this reform movement: the old city hall style of obsessive individualism must give way to the discipline of party; candidates must be elected on the basis of policy not personality; they must be accountable to the public on a continuing basis for implementing the programme on which they are elected. Over a century late, the issue of responsible government has finally been raised at the level of politics where citizen participation should be easiest to realize.

The 1969 election did more than commit two of the three national parties to active involvement in Toronto politics and define

From *The Canadian Forum*, February, 1970, pp. 262-63. Reprinted by permission.

an ideology of urban reform. It gave the parties an initial beach-head in both City Council and the Board of Education. Whatever can be said about the election results, they were hardly a "crushing rejection" of party politics by the voters. One in every two aldermanic votes cast was for the candidate of the Liberal or New Democratic parties. Six of the least progressive incumbents (all members of the Conservative party) lost their seats. Ten of the twenty-two aldermen in City Council are members of Civac, the N.D.P. and the Liberal party who have obtained half of the seats on the Executive, and three of the four standing committee chairmanships. Acting as an informal coalition, the reform-minded group have taken the initiative in establishing some new principles: that the Executive should be answerable to the Legislature; that Council should debate questions of principle, not just make decisions of administrative detail. The party-based reformers are in the process of changing the name of the political game in city hall from administration to government by representatives.

If J.G. were in closer touch with City Hall he would know that the reform coalition of which he speaks romantically as a possibility for the next election in 1972 was in fact a nascent reality a few days after the election – not as a fourth party but as a working alliance of the city parties, the reformist independents and the citizen groups that are actively concerned about the gut issues facing the city: the Spadina Expressway and spot re-zoning. Not that all problems of the city can be solved by his formula of radical conservatism. There are new social issues that call for creative action beyond a simple "Stop Progress" stance: transportation in the urban core, for example, or the social crisis of drug abuse. In any case the parties are alive and growing outside City Hall as well as inside. They have the next three years to prove that they are indeed relevant as channels for more effective citizen power in the city's political life.

Having annihilated party politics in his opening salvo, J.G. manages to make four serious claims about my own campaign in his next unargued sentence: that I was responsible for "ensuring the defeat" of Controller Margaret Campbell; that she was the "only alternative" to Dennison; that my own vote was insignificant; that in any case my campaign accomplished nothing. These charges demand some analysis.

To blame me for "ensuring" Margaret Campbell's defeat is to write history backwards. It assumes that there was a constant number of voters regardless of my campaign, that those 32,000 who voted for me would have voted had I not been a candidate and would have voted for Campbell, not Dennison. This arithmetic may be logical, but it isn't political. With the confusion of image and policy that characterized the campaign, it is highly unlikely that, had I not been a candidate, those 32,000 would have voted *en bloc* for Margaret Campbell, an official Conservative, rather than Bill Dennison, an official N.D.P. Despite his record in office of regressive conservatism, and despite my best efforts to bring out the close links between Dennison, the Conservative party and the big developers, the incumbent mayor managed nevertheless to salvage his attractiveness to many cautious voters. But the important point that J.G. had difficulty comprehending is the fact that I was a *party* candidate, nominated at a properly delegated convention of the Liberal ward associations. If I hadn't been nominated, someone else would have been the mayoralty candidate and fought the campaign on the progressive platform that the new party had spent eight months in developing. Were it not for the Toronto Labour Council's stubborn support of "Buffalo Bill," the N.D.P. would also have fielded a mayoralty candidate. J.G. would presumably have the N.D.P. equally responsible for the defeat of his "only alternative" had the results been the same.

If J.G. is saying that I could not seriously hope to be elected by the pothole and mill-rate voters in a fight against two incumbents, he is right. My campaign explicitly aimed at bringing out the "silent majority," the electorate who never voted in municipal elections. We acknowledged from the beginning that I needed at least a 50 per cent turnout to challenge the solid old city vote that the Dennison machine could pull out regardless of issue. That I got half as many votes as Dennison in a turnout that was lower than normal on a bitterly cold day indicates that I had made a greater impact on the traditional homeowner vote than expected.

My campaign didn't succeed in its primary objective, but it did accomplish two others. It turned the campaign into a policy debate rather than the traditional mudslinging based on personality. If J.G. had followed the campaign closely he would have seen that it was the Liberals who introduced into the election arena such issues as the scandalously inequitable state of the municipal franchise (on which the incumbents were silent), the social issue of drug abuse (that the Old Guard felt to be too hot to handle), and raised the long-range question of city power in dealing with such multi-jurisdictional problems as pollution and airport planning. On every policy issue from transportation to amalgamation, from electoral reform to tenants' rights, the platform I enunciated was more elaborate, more concrete and more radical than the positions taken by Mrs. Campbell, as my endorsements by both the *Globe and Mail* and the *Star* indicated.

A further achievement of the campaign is its impact on the thinking of the Liberal party federally and provincially. The Prime Minister's mind isn't changed by a single confrontation, but if he is hearing the voice of the cities with a new force it is largely because Liberals are using the policy-making process within the party, such as the Harrison conference, to urge Ottawa to reappraise its approach to the city. At the provincial level too, our city stands are forming the basis for Liberal policy. The creation of a three dimensional consciousness of the city's problems within the national parties is an essential prerequisite for educating the provincial and federal governments about the new city realities. But even here J.G. misses the point. An organizational shoring-up of the federal and provincial party organizations may be a useful by-product of the parties' entry into municipal politics. Far more important is the internal shift of power. The prospect that continuing involvement in the direct, participatory politics of the city can transform the national parties from campaign machines lying dormant between elections to permanently active vehicles for citizen participation remains the most hopeful aspect of the national parties.

A Reply to Stephen Clarkson

J.L.GRANATSTEIN

Stephen Clarkson apparently feels that my editorial on "The New City Politics" in the January issue was "like hearing a badly scratched record" of misconceptions about the last Toronto elections. I can understand Steve feeling that people had misconceptions about the role of political parties in municipal politics, especially considering the results of the voting, but I regret more than I can express that he is still unable to hear the music, no matter how badly scratched the record may be.

I wish that I had the space and the patience to deal *seriatim* with his remarks, but I do not. There are two major points that need to be answered, however.

In my editorial, I had raised the hope that in the next municipal election a genuine reformers' party would be in the race. Stephen Clarkson was helpful enough to point out that a coalition of reform aldermen is now in existence at City Hall. So it is – and hallelujah for that. But what will happen to this group at the next election? The N.D.P. aldermen will be opposed by the Grits. Sewell will be opposed by both N.D.P. and Liberal. We will be back in the destructive dogfight of the old party system, and the coalition of reformers will be destroyed on the rock of campaign bitterness. Surely the obvious and intelligent step is to bring all the reformers, whatever their federal or provincial allegiance, into a civic party. *That* is the new city politics.

Most important, Steve Clarkson did not seriously grapple with my central question: what are the advantages to the citizens of

From *The Canadian Forum*, March, 1970, p. 288. Reprinted by permission.

Toronto in having the national parties involved on the local scene? The only suggestion he ventured was that the municipal Liberals will make Pierre Trudeau hear "the voice of the cities." If Steve can believe that, he can believe anything – and obviously does. Clearly, Mr. Trudeau talks only to God. The disadvantage of the interjection of national parties into municipal politics, however, is clear. The Liberals, for example, are not a progressive party in Toronto, Mr. Clarkson notwithstanding. Hugh Bruce is a Liberal and so, for God's sake; is Allan Lamport. No party with such men can hope to be a reform party, and there have been no signs of any effort to re-make the party. The old parties would bring expensive campaigns in their train – and hence more reliance than ever on the developers' dollars. They would bring bigger and more efficient machines – and make it harder than ever to get rid of the Bruces and Lamports and their ilk. And most important they would probably divide up the reform vote – and that is something that we cannot afford.

Party politics failed in the last election, and Steve Clarkson's interpretations of the figures simply cannot alter that fact. He won a bare twenty per cent of the vote and ran a poor third. The party label candidates for alderman attracted only half the vote – and this despite the built-in recognition factor of the party name. If Clarkson doesn't recognize this failure, that is his problem. But some others can hear the music – and the record doesn't sound scratched at all. The new city politics, however, can only come if we begin planning now for the next election. Let's get a genuine reform party and take over City Hall lock, stock, and twin towers. Come home, Steve; there may even be a place for you.

Le cauchemar de Drapeau sera son nouveau défi

ALBERT TREMBLAY

Devant les caméras de la télévision, Jean Drapeau tire les conclusions du mandat «très clair» que vient de lui donner la population. Jean Drapeau est à nouveau maire de Montréal.

Il parle beaucoup d'autorité et peu de démocratie; il oublie ses collabórateurs et, dans cette euphorie d'une soirée d'élections, le nom du Parti civique est à peine évoqué. Depuis 1960, le scénario est le même. Il sera le même en ce dernier dimanche d'octobre.

A une énorme différence près: Jean Drapeau réélu, l'administration Drapeau-Saulnier n'en aura pas moins cessé d'exister.

Lucien Saulnier se sera retiré, laissant à Jean Drapeau seul la haute main sur l'administration d'une ville déjà si profondément marquée par la personnalité de deux hommes, différents au départ mais devenus presque semblables au bout de dix années de travail en commun.

Elections qui vont marquer la fin d'une époque et le début d'une autre. La fin d'une époque où, sans doute largement aidé par les circonstances, Jean Drapeau est vite devenu l'homme des grandes choses et des réalisations percutantes, tandis que, condamné dès le départ à concilier les grandes idées avec la réalité plus quotidienne des possibilités financières de Montréal, Lucien Saulnier faisait office d'administrateur.

Lucien Saulnier a donc décidé de «rentrer chez lui» Ce départ cadre mal avec le mode de travail du tandem: les «grandes choses» à peu près terminées, voici venue l'heure des problèmes administra-

From *Le Magazine Maclean*, Vol. 10, No. 2, February, 1970, pp. 11-19. Reprinted by permission.

tifs considérables qui s'ensuivent; il eut paru plus naturel que l'administrateur accepte alors de «garder le fort.»

Mais Lucien Saulnier a refusé de jouer ce rôle. Fatigué, un peu déçu de cette expérience de dix ans (il l'avoue franchement en conseillant à son entourage de ne jamais «faire de la politique»), il quitte peut-être parce qu'il exécuta beaucoup plus qu'il ne pensa.

Un jour peut-être, on saura ce que fût exactement ce mariage de raison entre deux hommes qui, si loin l'un de l'autre pourtant, ont toujours su projeter l'image de la parfaite harmonie.

Grâce à cette apparente harmonie, Montréal est devenue une véritable métropole mais qui, pour le demeurer, doit poursuivre son développement.

Or l'effritement de l'équipe Drapeau-Saulnier survient à une époque transitoire de la vie de Montréal où son développement, endiablé depuis quelques années, a besoin d'un temps de pose. Montréal cherche un peu son second souffle au milieu de gouvernements supérieurs qui prêchent l'austérité et d'une situation monétaire internationale qui exige des administrateurs une certaine retenue. Une telle période de «réflexion» donne toujours une impression «d'immobilisme,» surtout dans le cas de l'administration Drapeau-Saulnier alors que la «réflexion» arrive à l'heure où les «grands projets» sont terminés et où il reste à s'attaquer aux «petits»: comme la rénovation urbaine par exemple. C'est en faisant la somme des travaux et des réalisations de l'administration municipale que leaders syndicaux, dirigeants de certains corps intermédiaires et présidents des comités de citoyens ont dénoncé la présence immorale du taudis dans une ville qui continue encore, pour un temps, de fonctionner au rythme des réalisations spectaculaires.

L'ère du spectaculaire est pourtant bien révolue. Pour Drapeau, comme pour Saulnier, prolonger le métro ne sera jamais plus construire le métro. Dans cette optique, on voit mal le maire Jean Drapeau, qui risque fort en plus de se retrouver drôlement seul au lendemain des élections du 25 octobre: où trouvera-t-il donc un autre Lucien Saulnier?

Jean Drapeau dirige un parti politique juridiquement inexistant et se manifestant très peu, dont la «pensée» est souvent dirigée à partir du bureau obscur d'un homme méconnu même de ce parti: un ancien journaliste qui occupe la fonction officielle de chef de cabinet du maire, Charlie Roy. Un parti que Jean Drapeau a toujours voulu homogène: un parti «municipal» qui est soumis au culte du chef et qui, en silence, voue énormément de respect à Lucien Saulnier.

C'est à l'intérieur de ce parti, et plus probablement à l'intérieur du comité exécutif, que Jean Drapeau devra choisir l'éventuel successeur de Lucien Saulnier. L'évidente faiblesse de son parti ne lui facilitera pas les choses: il n'y a peut-être pas un montréalais sur 1,000 qui soit en mesure de nommer l'un ou l'autre des six membres du comité exécutif montréalais.

Jean Drapeau s'est donné une image. Celle de l'homme des grandes choses, des réalisations ou des déclarations fracassantes. Il a donné à la politique municipale une résonnance plus vaste que jamais. Ce n'est pas l'homme du «train-train» de la municipalité, des travaux d'aqueduc ou d'égout, de l'asphalte à refaire, de l'usine d'épuration à construire, des ordures à cueillir, de la rue à élargir ou des problèmes de circulation à résoudre.

Les affaires strictement municipales ont toujours été laissées à Lucien Saulnier. Même sans convention écrite (la Charte de Montréal ne précise pas que le maire est habilité à penser et le président de l'exécutif à exécuter), les journalistes et les membres du parti civique ont appris à force de «voyez M. Drapeau» ou de «voyez M. Saulnier» que l'administration municipale a toujours été très nettement séparée de la politique municipale, chasse gardée du maire Jean Drapeau.

A une exception près: les annexions.

La politique d'annexion de Montréal a été dirigée du bureau de Lucien Saulnier. Elle cadrait d'ailleurs mieux avec les préoccupations d'un administrateur, la nécessité «d'unifier les ressources» des municipalités de L' ile de Montréal découlant d'une kyrielle de problèmes administratifs. L'occasion était belle: Saulnier entra allègrement en politique, attaqua à tour de rôle gouvernement provincial et gouvernement fédéral.

Il se retire à l'instant précis où cette guerre de mots porte fruits: la «communautée urbaine» du ministre Lussier répond presque mot pour mot à la définition qu'en a faite Lucien Saulnier il y a plus de quatre ans. Majoritaire, et au conseil et à l'exécutif, il est normal de prévoir que cette ville unifiée au niveau des grandes préoccupations administratives va augmenter encore le fardeau administratif de la métropole en compliquant du même coup la tâche qui attend Jean Drapeau.

Car dans ce contexte d'une métropole appelée à dicter des politiques administratives à ses 28 voisines, le maire aura besoin d'un président d'exécutif extrêmement fort. Et remplacer Saulnier, ne sera pas chose facile: tenus à la stricte discipline du parti, les conseillers municipaux et les membres du comité exécutif (surtout ces derniers) n'ont vraiment eu aucune chance de se faire à la politique municipale; aucun des 48 membres du Parti civique n'a une réputation qui dépasse le cadre physique de l'hôtel de ville. Il lui faudra donc «bâtir» de toutes pièces ce futur président qui devra s'arroger, graduellement et à l'exemple de Saulnier, une part de plus en plus importante des responsabilités administratives; qui devra résister d'abord, puis s'accommoder ensuite, d'une politique émanant d'un homme pour qui l'autorité a toujours constitué le leitmotiv politique.

Adulé par des électeurs qui ne se formalisent pas des méthodes, Jean Drapeau manie, avec une étonnante dextérité, les concepts d'autorité et de démocratie. Il parvient à fondre les deux, tortures suffisamment les définitions pour en arriver à asseoir «sa» conception de la démocratie.

Homme d'action, il se formalise peu de changements d'orientation en cours de route, la politique devant, selon lui, laisser place à l'improvisation. Ses conceptions de la démocratie et de la politique lui rendent difficile la tâche de prévoir ce que sera le Montréal de demain à l'heure où il s'apprête, presque seul, à en définir et les formes et la vocation.

Coincé entre le besoin évident de protéger l'image de l'homme des grandes occasions et celui, plus rigide, de maintenir au niveau actuel le fardeau financier des contribuables, Jean Drapeau réagit à la façon de Jean Drapeau: il élude d'un trait le problème du quotidien en plaçant à l'enseigne d'une «politique de prolongement» toutes les questions impliquant des solutions purement administratives.

Puis il se choisit un nouveau défi. Et pour ajouter au piquant de la situation, il choisit précisément celui-là même qui a été à la source de ce premier mouvement d'opposition (dont il conteste d'ailleurs l'existence avec énergie).

Ce défi, ce sera la politique d'habitation de Montréal.

Jean Drapeau exulte:

«Les grands projets, les grandes réalisations, cela inclue l'habitation et dans cinq ans, Montréal sera en mesure de dire au monde de quelle façon il convient de faire de la rénovation urbaine. . . .»

«Faire de la rénovation à partir d'une formule «sans coeur,» c'est facile. J'ai déjà dit que notre programme d'habitations demanderait vingt ans d'efforts et des déboursés d'un milliard de dollars. Ce programme est bien lancé. Nous avons dû vaincre la résistance de milieux mieux nantis, mais le climat s'améliore et le rythme des travaux va aller s'accélérant. . . .»

Ce défi a quelques avantages; il répond au départ à ceux qui commencent à se poser des questions sur l'importance relative des politiques municipales; il autorise l'administration à parler encore de «grandes réalisations» à partir de réserves financières provenant en bonne partie des gouvernements fédéral et provincial; il permet en outre à Jean Drapeau de répondre à ceux qui lui ont imposé, entre deux règnes à l'hôtel de ville et à un moment où Jean Drapeau ne représentait pas l'autorité, ce projet d'habitations Jeanne-Mance, ce «plan Dozois» qui tranche la ville en deux, qui ne répond pas aux besoins réels et qui a été érigé sur des terrains «qu'il faudra bien un jour ou l'autre utiliser à d'autres fins.»

Maintenant que les grandes choses sont faites, Jean Drapeau a décidé que l'heure des défavorisés était (enfin! diront sans doute ceux qui se posent aujourd'hui des questions) venue.

La réponse s'appellera «Petite Bourgogne.» Il ne s'agit plus de construire une «réserve» à l'intention des défavorisés, mais de transformer un quartier existant sans déplacer ces défavorisés.

Si le projet est mirobolant, les travaux avancent lentement. Les comités de citoyens reprochent à l'administration un manque de consultation et un enthousiasme qui ne se traduit pas dans les faits.

Le manque apparent d'enthousiasme, Jean Drapeau l'explique par une certaine résistance des milieux mieux nantis. Il cite l'exemple de «l'Opération 300.» Il s'agissait de reloger temporairement les personnes déplacées par les travaux de réaménagement de la Petite Bourgogne dans d'autres secteurs de la métropole. «Nous avons été forcés de dépenser des mois d'énergie à convaincre des personnes, pas plus favorisées que celles impliquées, qu'il n'y avait aucun risque économique à vivre près de ces centres de relogement.» Les propriétaires craignaient que le voisinage de ces centres temporaires de logements destinés aux défavorisés fasse crouler la valeur de leurs propriétés.

Au niveau de la consultation, la réponse est plus évasive. Elle fait corps avec la conception que se fait Jean Drapeau de la démocratie. Un sujet que l'on aborde avec un peu d'appréhension, en s'attendant à voir bondir un homme qui a souvent été accusé de malmener la démocratie ou de ne pas y croire.

Jean Drapeau est pourtant heureux d'aborder le sujet. Il se décrit d'abord comme un fin démocrate avant d'expliquer que sa conception de la démocratie correspond à une «démocratie directe,» sans intermédiaire entre la masse et le sommet.

Une démocratie axée sur l'autorité, sur le besoin que ressent le peuple d'être dirigé et qui se traduit à peu près de la façon suivante: «Le peuple a toujours voulu un gouvernement fort, un gouvernement qui mène; il est fatigué d'une démocratie qui n'est faite que de discussions.»

Il s'agit donc de mettre en place un gouvernement fort, de donner à ce gouvernement un chef autoritaire. Ce chef soumet à la population un programme politique qui est ratifié le jour de l'élection. Le parti s'engage par la suite à ne pas déroger à ce programme.

Démocratie directe qui se passe des intermédiaires, des groupes de pression et de leaders syndicaux et qui écarte toute possibilité de «lobbying»: «Les hommes qui parlent au nom de 100,000 autres hommes, ça ne vaut tout simplement rien....» Si on insiste, il recourt à l'exemple: «Avez-vous déjà voté pour Marcel Pépin?»

Et si le parti déroge de son programme en cours de route? – Et si le parti est tellement fort qu'on en arrive, à toute fin pratique, à ne plus avoir d'elections? – Et si des événements imprévisibles font que la population elle-même finit par avoir envie de changer d'idée en cours de route?

Questions pertinentes lorsqu'on considère que depuis 1960, les campagnes électorales (municipales) n'ont certainement pas constitué une tribune valable, que le Parti civique n'a à peu près jamais eu à défendre un programme politique et que l'information en provenance de l'hôtel de ville n'a pas été de nature à faire réfléchir les administrés.

Jean Drapeau pense que les administrés et les corps intermédiaires ont la grande presse à leur disposition et qu'ils l'utilisent à profusion. «Les leaders syndicaux et les autres,» dira-t-il, «ont eu davantage de publicité gratuite au cours des dernières années que l'administration municipale.»

Reste aussi le «courrier du maire.» Jean Drapeau reçoit beaucoup de lettres. Il les lit toutes et c'est là, dit-il, qu'il perçoit le mieux le pouls de son peuple.

La majorité le suit et il gouverne pour la majorité.

Ainsi cette décision de «restreindre» le droit de manifester à Montréal. Jamais, une déclaration de Jean Drapeau n'aura fait couler autant d'encre.

Jean Drapeau ne s'en formalise pas. Dans son esprit, ce n'est pas la législation qui prête le flanc à la critique, c'est plus simplement, la nature du règlement qui a été mal comprise.

Expliqué par Jean Drapeau, ce règlement réaffirme le droit de manifester. Mais en interdisant les manifestations sur le domaine public, il met fin à une «espèce de tolérance.» Parce que l'utilisation du domaine public «à des fins autres que celles prévues à l'origine» n'est garantie par aucun texte de loi. Or, selon M. Drapeau tout au moins, les rues ont été conçues et réalisées pour le bien de la collectivité et dans le but premier de faire circuler des vêhicules. Les parcs ont été aménagés pour faire jouer les enfants et les édifices publics pour loger les services administratifs gouvernementaux.

Pour Jean Drapeau, le droit au domaine public est un droit sacré et ce droit appartient à la majorité. Le «droit acquis» (résultant de cette «certaine tolérance») n'existe pas davantage dans l'esprit du maire et, de toute façon, il lui apparaît évident que dans l'esprit de la très grande majorité, «les gens ont le droit de manifester à condition que ce soit dans la rue des autres. . . .»

Or, selon M. Drapeau, l'autorité existe pour garantir le droit de la majorité. Les antécédents (les «tolérances») s'expliquent par le fait, simple, que «tant qu'il n'y a pas de danger pour la majorité, le législateur est tenté d'interpréter largement la législation dont il dispose.»

Autorité que lui garantit le droit de la majorité; majorité qui soutient ce concept de démocratie directe et politique axée sur des événements absolument prévisibles. C'est à partir de ces données, mises au service d'un «bourreau de travail,» qu'il faut construire le Montréal de Jean Drapeau.

Quand on lui parle de «demain,» Jean Drapeau se retranche

derrière son traditionnel refus à jouer avec l'hypothèse et se replie sur une politique qui doit «laisser place à l'improvisation» (la bonne improvisation, lorsqu'elle répond à la définition qu'il en fait). Il surmonte par habitude les obstacles au fur et à mesure.

Cette façon d'administrer a un avantage évident: n'ayant jamais eu à dire au départ très clairement où il voulait aller, Jean Drapeau est toujours en mesure de crier «victoire» au moment où il arrive à quelque chose. Il fixe les priorités au gré des événements, puis fonce, en laissant à l'improvisation (la bonne toujours) le soin de déterminer quel sera exactement l'objectif.

Demain, c'est déjà l'hypothèse. Et l'avenir d'une ville implique celui de deux millions d'hommes, autant de «choses» imprévisibles.

Montreal Poor Challenge Mayor Drapeau's Regime

MARGARET DALY

In a dingy second-floor apartment in the working-class east-end district of St. Jacques, a small band of dedicated, overworked political organizers are spending their days and nights fighting to change the entire face of municipal politics in Montreal.

They are the permanent staff of the Front d'Action Politique (FRAP), which is providing the first organized opposition to the administration of Mayor Jean Drapeau's ten-year regime.

Since last May, FRAP has received widespread public attention as the left-wing municipal political party that claims wage-earners and the urban poor, who comprise the vast majority of Montreal's population, get no representation at city hall, where almost all the 52 council seats are held by the Civic Party of Mayor Drapeau and City Council President Lucien Saulnier.

Grandiose schemes

FRAP wants to see the city's priorities changed from grandiose development schemes and prestige projects like the Olympics, to such gut issues as housing, welfare, and health care.

Although the fledging party will not run a mayoralty candidate against Drapeau himself in the October 25 municipal elections, it will field 30 to 40 aldermanic candidates, in most of the city's 18 wards.

But FRAP – the initials are an acronym for the French slang to strike at something – is much more than a municipal electoral party.

From *Toronto Star*, September 12, 1970. Reprinted with permission *Toronto Daily Star*.

It was created as an umbrella group of the myriad citizens' committees and other community organizations which have sprung up in the past seven years or so to fight city hall.

FRAP's workers speak not of "the party" but of "the movement," and they are determined not to become mired in the traps of electoral politics. Already they are planning a "winter offensive" which will take place regardless of what happens at the polls October 25.

"How it got started was, the citizens' committees were getting stronger and stronger," explained FRAP vice-president Robert Lacaille, 39, a door-to-door bread salesman. "We've got 83 different citizens' committees in the central city. But every time you fight, you get only so far before you get blocked by city hall. They're the guys who have the decision-making power. So we had to face the fact that, until we get some of this power, no matter how hard we work we're not going to get much farther than we are now. Many of our people have been in these movements for several years. They don't have the temperament to keep waiting and waiting. So it was the natural thing that we should come to putting up our own candidates. But it's not the only thing, or even the most important thing," he added.

"The most important thing is getting the people involved in city politics. Drapeau and Saulnier, they run the city for a little minority of capitalists – the majority of the people get nothing."

A strong streak of anti-capitalism runs through FRAP's platform – much more so than is usual in politics at the municipal level.

The socio-economic situation in Montreal tends to contribute to this. Unlike Toronto's strongest citizens' movements, which have been middle-class – Stop Spadina – and mixed income – Don Vale Residents' Association – as well as low-income, the citizens' committees here are made up mostly of working-class people and welfare recipients.

Low Wages

Middle-income Montrealers tend to cluster in Outremont, Westmount, and the town of Mount Royal, which are not part of the city, and in the suburbs. Half the city's wage earners make less than $3,550 a year.

In Toronto the split of tenants to homeowners is about 40-60. Here about 85 per cent of the city's residents are tenants. And this is the first civic election in which non-property owners have been allowed to vote.

Thus the Drapeau-Saulnier administration represents about 15 per cent of the Montreal populace, say FRAP officials, and only a third of these turned out to vote in the last civic election in 1966. Fifty of the 52 city councillors are professionals or businessmen.

"Drapeau made his name in the rest of Canada with the big building boom and all the rest of it," said Henri Sirois, "but there's another side to that story that the people don't hear so much about."

Sirois, a factory worker, was driving through Ste. Anne ward, where he is running as a FRAP candidate. It covers south-central Montreal, including most of the downtown area.

"There's the Place Ville Marie, for example," he said with a gesture toward it. "That's in Ste. Anne ward. Two thousand housing units came down for that one.

"In those days they just sent you a piece of paper and you were out on the street. Today they put it in the newspapers and everything, so you can fight it a bit before you're thrown out.

"Over here is where 3,000 houses were torn down for parking lots for Expo '67, and the Autostade, where they play about six football games a year," he said.

"Now he's going to tear down 3,400 homes in the east for the Jeux Olympiques. He says he's going to build 3,000 for housing the athletes, which will later become low-cost housing for the people, but he doesn't talk about the 3,400 he's tearing down.

High Rents

"And Habitat at Expo, that was supposed to be low-cost housing after the fair was over. Rents there start at $260 a month for one bedroom."

FRAP estimates that the Drapeau administration has averaged about 2,000 dwelling units demolished each year. In 10 years it has provided 2,237 units of low-income public housing, most of these renovations of existing buildings.

The party's platform calls for the construction of at least 10,000 units a year and citizen participation in mass renovation of old but still good housing.

It also calls for the construction of public health clinics in the city's poorer districts, to be administered jointly by citizens of the districts and clinic staffs, re-organization and greater citizen participation in welfare services, free public transit as a long-term objective, and vast improvements in the parks and recreation programs for the poor districts.

Mayor Drapeau has been quoted as saying the city's recreation budget for the next six years will go to finance the Olympics.

Taken as a whole, the FRAP program sounds idealistic, to say the least, but many of its planks spring from ideas the citizens' groups have already experimented with.

A community-run health clinic is a reality in St. Jacques ward – in fact, it occupies the same building as the FRAP headquarters. Welfare rights organizations, which have sprung up in several parts of the city, have won major concessions from both city and provincial welfare officials, and have become among the strongest of the citizens' committees.

Drive for Members

The citizens' committees will probably provide the major support for the new party in the coming months. At present FRAP's direct, card-carrying membership is between 800 and 1,000, although it has not yet held any sort of membership drive, and plans to launch one shortly. But through the committees it has lines to several hundred more people.

It also has the support of the central council of the Confederation of National Trade Unions (CNTU), the separatist Parti Quebecois, and the provincial New Democratic Party (such as it exists in Quebec).

The labor alliance is a significant one, for in the early days of the citizens' movement, there was considerable distrust between it and organized labor. Many of the district "workers' committees" were made up mainly of unorganized laborers, and their militant actions sometimes put them in conflict with the unions.

In fact, the more conservative QFL, Quebec Federation of Labor (the provincial arm of the Canadian Labor Congress, whose members are mainly the big American unions) has not officially endorsed FRAP, although many of its members are active in the party.

Their main point of contention is that FRAP opposes the multi-million dollar Concordia Estates development, which will demolish hundreds of homes in the city's Milton Park area and which a strong citizens' committee has been fighting for two years.

The QFL's construction unions, not unnaturally, support the development. This is the sort of position which makes non-union workers and the many student activists who also work for FRAP, cynical about unions.

But the CNTU, much more militant and left wing than the QFL, has been organizing for three years now on what it calls the "second front" – fighting for its members' rights as citizens and consumers, as well as workers – and its good will seems to have been accepted by most FRAP workers.

They consider unionized labor a relatively privileged group (about 30 per cent of Montreal's workers are unionized), but necessary to a mass movement.

"The program of FRAP is the same as the program of the central council of the CNTU, which was voted on by the council's 67,000 members," said Jean-Yves Vezina, who works for the central council as a co-ordinator of political action. "It was logical the council should get behind FRAP.

"Before FRAP, the central council never thought of doing anything at the municipal level, but it's important. It is a level where you can get to many people and politicize them. The issues are very concrete, quickly and easily understood, and they affect people directly."

Vezina, 27, has been assigned by the central council to work full-time for FRAP during the municipal election campaign.

"How well we do depends on how much of an organization the Parti Quebecois will give us," Vezina said. The area he is working in elected one Parti Quebecois MLA and two Liberals provincially, and has a strong PQ organization.

But it also includes the pocket of English-speaking people considered responsible for the defeat of René Lèvesque, PQ leader.

"It's impossible to do this mass election organizing in a month, without resources. This is why we say to organizations like the PQ don't pass resolutions supporting us. Give us your street organizers.

"The electoral system is all just a big game anyway, but if you're going to play it, you have to play it correctly. A lot of people in the CAPs" (the Comités d'Action Politique, the individual ward organizations that make up FRAP) "were against contesting this municipal election at all because they don't believe too much in elections," he said.

"Me, I feel we must go through this electoral bit again. We need a few more examples to show people how unfair the whole system is. The top level people in the Parti Quebecois believe in it, but even they are starting to question it all. Why not, when in the recent provincial election they get a quarter of the vote, and only a handful of seats in the legislature?

"So we'll give North American democracy one more chance."

At least 90 per cent of FRAP's membership is separatist, in the estimation of the party's president, Paul Cliche, a 35-year-old former journalist and trade unionist. Its image is undoubtedly one reason it has had difficulties attracting even the more progressive elements of the city's English-speaking population.

"The English newspapers like to make a very big deal out of the fact that we are supported by the Parti Quebecois," said Cliche. "We are also supported by the NDP, we have very many Liberals who are active in our organization, we'll take support from who ever wants to give it."

A Separatist

Cliche himself is a separatist, but considers that the subject is not one on which FRAP should take a position, since it has nothing to do with municipal priorities.

At the FRAP convention that elected him president a couple of weeks ago, he said: "It is more important to find ways to give the majority of citizens power than to discuss the global future of Quebec."

"At present one of our most important functions is to give the people information, so they can make important decisions," said Rene Denis, 24, one of the organizers on FRAP's permanent staff. (Like all the permanent staff, he makes $95 a week, raised through donations.)

"This is one of the reasons why it doesn't matter if we elect only three or four members to the city council. They can still obtain the information and it is the FRAP's job to give it to the people. Then the people can decide for themselves whether they want the Olympics or low-cost housing – or what the future of Quebec should be, for that matter."

"Me, how I got involved, was I got expropriated three times," said Robert Lacaille. "Once in 1966 for the Trans-Canada Highway, which they still haven't built, then again for the highway in 1968, and now this year for public housing."

Lacaille lives in the city's Little Burgundy district, where some of the earliest citizens' committees fought for citizen participation in urban renewal.

"I started going to the committee meetings, and the first thing you know I'm into everything. My wife, Rose, was the Parti Quebecois candidate for our riding in the last election.

"Often I get mad when I see all the other guys like me, with kids and all, who don't get involved. If you don't want to change things in the city for your own sake, you should want to for your kids' sake.

"But that's the real purpose of the FRAP – to get these people involved. Drapeau and Saulnier have kept them asleep for 10 years, but they're starting to wake up now."

3

Recruitment and Political Perceptions of Urban Politicians

Introduction

The degree to which political parties are active in a city is to a considerable degree a reflection of the prevailing political culture of that community. This political culture, in turn, is moulded by the orientation of the political élite in each community, including the elected officials. Some understanding of this process is provided by the following articles examining the pattern of recruitment and political values of local decision-makers. Comparing the background and orientations of urban politicians with the community at large provides some clues as to why party-like functions are performed in some cities but not others – and performed in different degrees in different communities.

In the first article, Guy Bourassa gives a detailed historical account of recruitment patterns in the city of Montreal. He accounts for the changes in council composition from the English speaking élite to the predominance of middle-class French-speaking officials, many of whom make use of city hall as a stepping-stone to provincial politics.

Robert Easton and Paul Tennant provide further insight into the social composition of the civic political élite in their study of the embryonic party system in Vancouver. They then weave this into an examination of both the politicos' ideology and their outlook on a number of civic issues. Of special interest in their multi-faceted analysis is an examination of provincial party identification of local party leaders.

In the concluding selection, Alan Alexander compares the individual attributes of councilmen in Fort William and Port Arthur with the electorate of those cities. He finds that although many councillors hold memberships in senior political parties, they do not carry this identification into "nonpartisan" civic politics. Alexander surmises, on the basis of his findings, that the absence of a party system both increases the distance between the citizenry and the decision-maker and concommitantly diminishes the citizen's ability to influence his elected representative.

Les Élites politiques de Montréal: de l'aristocratie à la démocratie

GUY BOURASSA

Cette étude s'inscrit dans le cadre plus large d'une analyse de la vie politique montréalaise. Vouloir répondre à la question «qui gouverne?» exige que l'on considère d'abord les détenteurs officiels de la puissance politique. L'objectif à long terme que nous poursuivons amènera ensuite à tâcher de saisir le processus en action, à cerner les rôles et combats réels au moment de la mise en train d'actions importantes, de la prise de décision.[1] Pour le moment, la recherche présentée ici porte sur un aspect très précis: la connaissance des élites politiques officielles entre 1840 et 1960.

Montréal reçoit sa première charte municipale en 1833 mais son autonomie, tout au moins formelle, ne sera acquise pour de bon qu'en 1840. Entre cette date et 1960, trente-huit maires ont dirigé près d'une centaine de conseils municipaux. Voilà donc un personnel politique de bonne dimension. Qui ont été ces élus du peuple depuis cent-vingt ans? A quels groupes ethniques appartenaient-ils, à quelle religion; quel était leur statut social: leur occupation, leur niveau d'instruction; ont-ils participé à la politique à d'autres niveaux, provincial ou fédéral, sous quelle bannière? Telles sont les questions que nous nous sommes posées. Les éléments de réponse ont pu en général être obtenus et une forte majorité de ces élus possède une fiche à peu près complète. Les sources sont assez diverses, mais les dossiers d'archives en constituent l'essentiel. Mentionnons tout de

From *Canadian Journal of Economics and Political Science*, Vol. 31, (February, 1965), pp. 35-51. Reprinted by permission of the author and the *Journal*.

[1] Diverses recherches récentes nous ont été utiles dans cette perspective mais il faut faire une mention spéciale de R. A. Dahl, *Who Governs?* (New Haven: 1961).

même quelques recueils biographiques qui ont été précieux.[2] Voilà d'ailleurs un des aspects les plus étudiés de notre vie politique, grâce d'ailleurs à des recherches patientes et tenaces. Nous avons eu à les compléter dans le cas de conseillers municipaux surtout, et encore davantage à les soumettre à des analyses propres à la science politique. Au niveau d l'explication des tendances qui donnent une forme à cette histoire, plusieurs facteurs ont été cités: la croissance de la ville, la poussée démographique, les groupes ethniques, la modification dans les ressources politiques, etc. Sans établir de causalité stricte, notre analyse veut faire ressortir des corrélations significatives. Elles ne furent établies qu'après les avoir examinées sous plusieurs angles. Les comparaisons dans le temps se sont avérées particulièrement précieuses. Faut-il préciser que ces résultats participent à des concordances que d'autres ont précisées pour l'ensemble de la société canadienne française et aussi pour des communautés très différentes, notamment aux Etats-Unis. En tout cas, on ne peut que souhaiter que d'autres travaux viennent compléter et enrichir les «lois» qu'on peut déjà dessiner.

Précisons d'abord les grands traits de l'histoire du régime municipal montréalais. Cette tâche n'est guère facile puisqu'ici les formes les plus diverses chevauchent et s'entremêlent.

Du régime français, retenons que Montréal est érigée en ville libre en 1642, qu'elle le restera jusqu'en 1693 après quoi la tutelle du gouvernement de Québec sera entière. Il y a une absence quasi-totale d'institutions démocratiques à cette époque. Le changement de régime qui suit la conquête n'apporte d'ailleurs aucune modification majeure à cette situation. Il faudra attendre encore soixante-dix ans. Au tiers du dix-neuvième siècle, les Montréalais, conscients de leur nombre et aussi de leurs problèmes, veulent prendre leurs destinées en mains. Le gouvernement provincial accorde une charte en 1832, la retire en 1836, et la donne pour de bon en 1840.

Distinguons trois grandes périodes pour introduire un peu de clarté dans l'histoire des cent vingt ans qui suivent. De 1840 à 1900, un premier moment se caractérise par le fonctionnement régulier du jeu des élections. C'est l'époque où Montréal prend son essor. Une seconde tranche va du début du vingtième siècle jusqu'à 1943, faite

[2] F. J. Audet, *Les Députés de Montréal, 1792-1867* (Montréal: 1943); J. C. Lamothe, *Histoire de la corporation de Montréal* (Montréal: 1903).

de troubles, de mise en tutelle et marquée aussi par l'apparition de certains leaders de premier plan. L'électeur montréalais conserve au cours de ces années la possibilité de choisir ses représentants mais ceux-ci sont souvent réduits à l'inaction. Enfin, depuis vingt ans, le régime démocratique a reconquis tous ses privilèges. Depuis cette date, le suffrage est universel et l'on sait l'orientation de type parlementaire donnée récemment à la vie montréalaise.

Une Oligarchie éphémère

Montréal reçoit donc sa première charte le premier juin 1832. Cette charte était octroyée pour quatre ans et stipulait que seize représentants seraient élus.

La première élection eut donc lieu le premier juin 1833 et, le cinq suivant, les seize choisissaient le premier maire. Sur ce premier Conseil municipal, il y a peu de choses à mentionner. Retenons que la majorité est de langue anglaise, ce qui se reproduira aux élections de 1834 et 1835. Bon nombre de ces premiers élus reviendront à la politique municipale après la coupure des années 1836 à 1840.

Le premier maire de Montréal mérite une place à part. Jacques Viger a en effet été à la fois journaliste, écrivain, et surtout historien: il fonde en 1858 la Société Historique de Montréal et réunit en une oeuvre monumentale quarante-quatre tomes sur l'histoire du pays. Il fut aussi élu député en 1856.

La charte ne fut pas renouvelée en 1836: les troubles qui s'annonçaient et l'insécurité de l'époque poussèrent les dirigeants provinciaux à rendre le pouvoir aux juges de paix. Ils furent une cinquantaine dont seulement le tiers était d'origine française.

Toute cette époque a ses caractéristiques propres. Elle n'était guère favorable à la mise en place d'institutions démocratiques. La lutte entre les deux principaux groupes ethniques façonne aussi le système montréalais. Les représentants du peuple demeurent une caste plutôt fermée où l'anglo-saxon occupe l'échelon élevé. On voit d'ailleurs mal comment il aurait pu en être autrement au moment même où une vaste politique d'assimilation prenait forme. Bref, Montréal reste encore sous la tutelle québecoise et n'a pas encore donné naissance à un personnel politique original. L'an 1840 va cependant marquer le retour définitif du régime municipal.

1840-1873: Une aristocratie financière

En 1841, les montréalais élisent les membres du Conseil municipal. On notera pourtant que le maire restera choisi parmi les conseillers eux-mêmes pendant dix ans encore. L'essentiel reste que pour les trente ans à venir Montréal sera dirigée surtout par une équipe d'hommes d'affaires, parvenus par leur seule force à une prospérité remarquable. Des exceptions existent: celle entr'autres de Wolfred Nelson, modeste médecin qui prit une part importante aux Troubles de 1837; celle aussi de Édouard Raymond Fabre, lui aussi engagé dans ces luttes et tourné vers le commerce de la librairie et le journalisme.

Mais en gros, le pouvoir politique va être lié jusqu'en 1873 à la puissance financière. Ses représentants forment une élite homogène et fermée. La voie vers le gouvernement passe par le succès dans les affaires. La richesse constitue la ressource politique fondamentale: elle confère un statut social élevé et le droit de diriger. A cette époque, d'autres ressources, qui allaient acquérir un poids majeur, ne comptent guère. Le niveau d'instruction se situe plutôt bas. Peu de Montréalais peuvent alors poursuivre des études prolongées et les professionnels ne constituent qu'une minorité. D'autre part, le soutien du grand nombre importe peu ici. On retrouve les mêmes hommes aux divers postes-clés et ils n'ont pas à se soucier de l'appui massif du peuple. Ce trait ne se manifestera qu'au début du vingtième siècle. Bien entendu, tout cela signifie que la popularité des élus municipaux montréalais conserve une cote qui paraît aujourd'hui négligeable. Pour diverses raisons que nous allons approfondir, le peuple de Montréal se désintéresse assez largement de la chose publique pour laisser à ceux qui ont réussi en affaires le loisir de parachever leur démarche triomphale jusque sur la scène politique. . . .

James Ferrier, qui fut maire en 1845 et 1846, représente le cas typique de ce leader. Né à l'étranger, il émigre jeune et sans moyens. Après avoir fait rapidement sa fortune, il se lance dans la politique pour être successivement conseiller municipal, maire, conseiller législatif, puis sénateur. On pourrait aisément multiplier les descriptions de ce genre.

La prépondérance des hommes d'affaires est indiscutable. Des onze maires qu'a eus Montréal pendant ces trois décennies, neuf appartiennent au groupe des grands administrateurs, industriels et marchands, contre seulement deux professionnels – l'un avocat, l'autre médecin; et il faut faire exception pour Charles-Séraphin Rodier qui, bien que reçu avocat, pratiqua fort peu le droit pour s'adonner plutôt au commerce d'importation. Ce premier trait va de pair avec le faible degré d'instruction: quatre maires n'ont pas dépassé le niveau primaire et quatre autres ont reçu une formation secondaire.

On aperçoit le même phénomène chez les conseillers eux-mêmes. Les administrateurs, petits ou grands, chefs d'entreprise ou titulaires de postes élevés, constituent les deux tiers de ceux-ci et les professionnels ne forment là encore qu'une faible minorité, environ 15 pour cent. Ici aussi, le succès a été durement gagné et les esprits audacieux ont conquis droit de cité, au sens le plus strict. On passe aisément du commerce à la direction de la chose publique.

On peut déjà entrevoir le poids de l'origine ethnique dans cette classe dirigeante. Les Canadiens français occupent une place secondaire. Une certaine loi d'alternance, fréquemment voilée de toutes façons, fait bien qu'à un maire canadien anglais succède un maire canadien français. La règle vaudra plus ou moins jusqu'en 1914. Mais, à cette époque du moins, elle ne rend pas une image réelle de l'importance des divers groupes ethniques. En effet, s'il y a eu six maires d'origine française, soit un peu plus de la moitié, le conseil reste composé dans une proportion de 60 pour cent d'anglo-saxons, parmi lesquels les Écossais occupent une place à part. Il n'est pas inutile de rappeler, dans la perspective d'un rapprochement qu'il faudrait pouvoir approfondir, que les deux premiers députés élus par les Montréalais après l'Union étaient de langue anglaise, c'est-à-dire Benjamin Holmes et George Moffat.

Ce qui amène des remarques du même genre pour le lien religieux. On dispose ici de statistiques précises qui montrent que les catholiques romains représentent moins de la moitié des conseillers de cette période. L'explication majeure d'une telle situation relève de la structure démographique générale de Montréal au milieu du dix-neuvième siècle. Les Canadiens anglais ont longtemps été majoritaires. Nous reviendrons bientôt sur le facteur démographique.

Il serait pourtant erroné de conclure à l'absence des Canadiens français dans la vie municipale du temps. Le seul nom du premier maire de Montréal à détenir plus de cinq mandats (il en a en fait dix à son crédit, ce qui le place parmi les tout premiers) suffit à nuancer le tableau. Le carrière de l'honorable Jean-Louis Beaudry, qui fut d'abord élu dans les années qui ont précédé la Confédération, le démontre en effet très nettement. Les traits de cette carrière permettent aussi d'accentuer le portrait que nous sommes en train d'esquisser. Même modèle: origine modeste, succès financiers, longue carrière politique.

A propos des relations ethniques, il faut peut-être surtout prendre acte d'une évolution, lente à s'annoncer, mais qui allait réorienter profondément toute la situation. Au cours de ces années, les Canadiens français sont devenus la majorité dans la ville et si un nouvel aménagement des forces politiques ne fut réalisé que plus tard, peut-être même seulement au vingtième siècle, l'observateur peut percevoir les premiers craquements dès la seconde période que nous avons découpée.

Les remarques sur l'origine ethnique mettent en relief un autre trait de la vie politique municipale du temps, c'est-à-dire l'immense proportion de non-montréalais d'origine dans cette élite. Vers 1850 à 1860, Montréal prenait son essor et, très normalement, attirait des ruraux et des étrangers en grand nombre. C'est ainsi qu'à ses débuts, contrairement à ce qui se passe depuis cinquante ans, Montréal a été administrée par des hommes nés en dehors de ses limites: forte proportion d'immigrés d'abord et parmi ceux-ci prédominance des Écossais. Trois des premiers maires de Montréal sont ainsi nés en Écosse. Chez les conseillers même caractéristique: c'est pendant la décennie qui suit 1860 que leur proportion a été la plus élevée. Les Irlandais suivent de près au Conseil quoiqu'un seul maire fut originaire d'Irlande pendant cette période. Les autres groupes ethniques sont inexistants avant 1870, sauf une fraction infime de Juifs.

En second lieu, parmi les citoyens nés au Canada, la très grande majorité va du côté de ceux qui ne sont pas issus de souche montréalaise. Entre 1842 et 1873, deux maires seulement sont des montréalais de naissance: Wolfred Nelson et Charles-Séraphin Rodier dont nous avons déjà fait mention. Les autres viennent de la Province de Québec (Rivière du Loup, Sainte-Anne-des-Plaines), de l'Ontario (Amherstburg, Kingston) ou encore des États-Unis (John Easton Mills qui fut maire en 1847). La même tendance existera jusqu'au tournant du siècle puisqu'en 1900 seulement trois des vingt-cinq maires de Montréal sont nés dans cette ville. Le trait est peut-être encore plus accentué parmi les conseillers car il faut attendre 1950 pour voir plus de la moitié être originaire de Montréal. Pour la période qui nous occupe, la proportion de ceux-ci varie entre 30 et 40 pour cent.

Dernière particularité de cette première forme de l'élite politique montréalaise: son engagement politique, non pas que cet engagement fut en lui-même plus ou moins accentué. De tout temps, le lien entre la politique municipale et la politique provinciale ou fédérale a été puissant dans la vie montréalaise et les mêmes hommes passent d'un secteur à l'autre, ou même cumulent divers postes, avec la plus grande facilité. On distingue plutôt l'engagement de ces hommes par une allure profondément différente de celui de la catégorie qui suit. Peu en effet sont parvenus entre 1840 et 1873 à la politique provinciale ou fédérale par l'élection. Par exemple, deux maires ont été députés alors que le nombre des sénateurs et surtout des conseillers législatifs est élevé, environ une demi-douzaine pour ces derniers. Peut-on conclure de là qu'à cette époque l'entrée dans une autre arène politique se présentait surtout comme le couronnement d'une carrière et non comme une action parmi plusieurs autres vers une carrière publique? On serait porté à l'affirmer davantage quand on remarque que les conseillers municipaux aussi n'ont pas tellement opté pour la députation et que ceux qui sont devenus conseillers législatifs forment un groupe important. Pour être plus complet il importerait de tenir aussi compte de la structure même de la carte électorale de l'époque: les postes étaient peu nombreux et l'avènement de la Confédération avec les nouvelles divisions qu'elle allait entraîner va causer une modification que nous examinerons plus loin.

Comment expliquer l'existence à cette époque d'une élite montréalaise largement importée, surtout anglo-saxonne, et dominée par les milieux d'affaires? Quatre facteurs paraissent se détacher: (a) la situation d'ensemble de la vie politique canadienne à cette époque, (b) l'évolution de la ville – le fait qu'elle n'est encore qu'une petite ville, (c) l'absence d'une véritable tradition démocratique, (d) le système électoral lui-même: le scrutin public et les qualifications très lourdes qui sont requises aussi bien de l'électeur que de l'élu.

(a) Les années que nous venons d'examiner sont celles qui ont suivi l'Union et celles qui ont préparé la Confédération. L'année 1837 n'est pas loin et l'incendie de l'Hôtel du gouvernement en 1849 à Montréal montre assez le climat de l'époque. Comment pouvait être possible après les années tumultueuses entre 1830 et 1840 l'éclosion d'une véritable vie politique municipale? D'autres traits plus profonds, démographiques, raciaux, religieux, économiques, se dessinaient lentement pour façonner les limites du débat des années soixante. Après 1867 la scène montréalaise se verra mieux circonscrite et l'on peut dire qu'à ce moment apparaissent déjà les composantes d'une dynamique qui se déroule depuis.

(b) Ensuite, Montréal entre 1840 et 1870 est une ville qui bâtit ses assises. La croissance démographique le montre d'abord: elle franchit le cap des 100,000 habitants vers 1865. Le progrès économique prend lentement forme malgré les avatars des relations avec les voisins américains. Le port de Montréal se développe pour de bon à partir de 1850. Sur le plan politique, la ville qui a été la capitale, le centre nerveux du pays, est devenue simplement une entité parmi d'autres.

Tout cela donnait évidemment un ton et une allure bien particuliers à la politique municipale. Celle-ci ne tourne guère autour de grandes questions, il a'agit avant tout de donner à cette ville les moyens matériels, parfois les plus élémentaires, pour assurer sa croissance. A ce moment, le Conseil n'était tenu de se réunir que quatre fois l'an.

(c) A ces deux facteurs s'allient une ignorance profonde des mécanismes de la démocratie et le détachement inévitable d'une population qui n'a jamais eu l'occasion de les utiliser. Les exigences et les possibilités de cette nouvelle forme de vie politique restaient inconnues. Un tel vide s'accompagne en général d'un sérieux désintéressement vis-à-vis toute la vie politique, désintéressement qui a aussi ses racines dans les crises de la période dont les solutions ne sont guère proposées au peuple pour qu'il se détermine.

(d) Enfin, le système électoral lui-même était peu propice à la participation de l'ensemble de la population. Non seulement pour être candidat mais pour pouvoir voter se dressait une solide bannière financière. Ces règles dureront longtemps dans l'ensemble puisque le véritable changement n'aura lieu qu'en 1910. Jusqu'en 1889, le vote sera public. On imagine aisément les pressions de toutes sortes qui peuvent découler d'une telle procédure et les difficultés faites à ceux qui seraient tentés de s'opposer à la puissance financière. En même temps, le suffrage est loin d'être universel: seuls les hommes sont électeurs et éligibles. Comment alors s'étonner des particularités de la vie politique du temps? Pourtant, certains phénomènes prenaient forme qui étaient sur le point de soumettre la structure de la vie politique montréalaise à une profonde mutation longue de quarante ans.

1873-1914: L'éclatement d'une élite

En 1875, un médecin de réputation internationale est élu maire; en 1885 on trouve à la tête de la ville de Montréal celui qui fonda *La Patrie* après avoir combattu au Mexique dans l'armée française; lui succède un avocat qui allait devenir premier ministre du Canada. L'homogénéité de l'élite qui avait dirigé Montréal jusqu'ici est brisée. La période qui s'ouvre est celle de la transition: les forces sont entremêlées, des leaders d'un nouveau type apparaissent en même temps que de puissants hommes d'affaires se font encore élire. Néanmoins de tout ce réseau de tendances se dégage progressivement une ligne de force qui va infléchir dans un sens nouveau la vie politique municipale pour parvenir à lui donner une allure bien marquée pendant la troisième période que nous avons découpée et qui s'ouvre avec la Première Guerre Mondiale.

En tant que ressource politique, l'argent ne détient plus de monopole. Il n'est pas davantage la seule base du prestige social. Le rayonnement intellectuel, le nombre et la puissance ethnique, deviennent des atouts de première force. Pour les années à venir, ces quatre types de capital politique auront de l'importance.

Dix-huit maires ont été élus pendant ces quarante ans. Pour certains, la renommée intellectuelle a été la base du pouvoir. Considérons par exemple la carrière de Sir William Hingston. Né de parents irlandais en 1829, au moment où Montréal était en train de conquérir le régime municipal, il fait de longues études de médecine à McGill University d'abord, puis à Edimbourg, en France, et en Allemagne. Sa carrière scientifique est remarquable: l'histoire de la chirurgie canadienne, écrit un commentateur, commence avec lui. C'est la première fois que Montréal se donne pour maire une personnalité de ce type, un grand universitaire. La politique attire des hommes nouveaux. Sir William Hingston s'est présenté aux Communes en 1875, il a été défait, mais il est nommé sénateur en 1896. D'autre part son activité intellectuelle ne l'empêche pas de s'occuper des affaires; il préside entr'autres le «Montreal City and District Savings Bank.»

Trente-cinq ans plus tard on retrouve à peu près la même carrière dans la biographie du maire John James Guérin, Canadien anglais, fils d'un professeur de McGill University, ce maire fut lui aussi un universitaire qui occupa de hautes charges dans sa profession. Ici encore les affaires occupent une bonne place. Sa carrière politique fut cependant plus large et mieux réussie: élu à l'Assemblée législative, ministre sans portefeuille, il passera à la Chambre des Communes en 1925 pour se retirer définitivement en 1930 après une défaite.

Un facteur semble pourtant avoir marqué cette évolution plus que tout autre: la poussée démographique d'abord, la conquête d'un statut majoritaire par les Canadiens français au sein de la population de Montréal et dans ses structures politiques. A notre avis, on ne saurait guère exagérer le retentissement de cette progression. Nous y reviendrons à diverses reprises car nous croyons être en présence, dans ce cas, d'un des plus puissants leviers qui ont donné son orientation à la vie politique de Montréal.

L'évolution de la population de Montréal depuis 1851 se caractérise par un rapide accroissement, qui va même jusqu'à doubler le chiffre total entre 1851 et 1871, soutenu presqu'à ce rythme pendant quelques décennies pour finalement accuser un certain ralentissement, surtout depuis 1931.

Cette expansion qui a fait passer la population montréalaise, au cours de notre seconde tranche, de 130,000 à 490,000 s'accompagne d'une évolution majeure dans la force respective des groupes ethniques. Pour les vingt années qui ont précédé 1871, les recensements soulignent la progression de l'élément francophone: il passe ainsi d'une proportion de 75 pour cent à près de 80 pour cent entre 1851 et 1871, dans l'ensemble de la province. A Montréal, le début de cette période marque une prépondérance des Canadiens anglais. En 1848, la proportion est de cinq contre quatre Canadiens français. Jean Bruchési note aussi que de 1840 à 1865 la population de la ville même de Montréal fut en majorité de langue anglaise.[3] A partir de 1871, la poussée démographique montréalaise ira de pair

[3]J. Bruchési, «Histoire économique,» dans *Montréal Économique* (Montréal: École des Hautes Études Commerciales, 1943), p. 29.

avec une implantation de plus en plus solide de l'élément canadien français.

Tableau 1. Évolution (en pourcentage) des principaux groupes ethniques dans l'Ile de Montréal, 1871-1951*

	1871	1881	1901	1911	1921	1931	1941	1951
Français	60,3	62,1	63,9	62,7	60,7	60,2	62,6	63,8
Anglais	38,1	35,2	33,7	26,2	27,3	26,3	24,2	22,2
Juifs	—	0,1	1,9	5,2	6,3	5,8	5,7	5,4
Italiens	0,1	0,2	0,5	1,3	2,0	2,2	2,3	2,3
Polonais	0,1	0,5	—	0,5	0,4	0,8	0,7	1,0

* N. Lacoste, *Les Caractéristiques sociales de la population du grand Montréal* (Montréal, 1958), p. 77.

Le tableau fait ressortir la stabilité de la proportion de l'élément français avec un certain mouvement vers la hausse, en même temps qu'un recul évident de l'élément canadien anglais pendant que deux autres groupes, les Juifs et les Italiens, fixent lentement leurs assises.

En même temps que s'organisent ces modifications fondamentales et sous leur poussée, le système électoral se modifiait à Montréal. On a déjà dit que le vote est devenu secret en 1889, ce qui ne peut manquer d'influencer, à long terme du moins, l'expression des diverses tendances. Il sera accordé aussi à une population plus large. La même année, les veuves ou les filles majeures sont admises au scrutin. En 1889, ce sera au tour des fonctionnaires de devenir citoyens à part entière. Enfin, les élections deviennent plus espacées, ce qui donne à la fois plus de prestige aux élus et élimine ce que pourrait avoir de routinier et même d'importun un rite répété d'année en année.

Toutes les barrières ne sont pourtant pas renversées puisqu'en 1899 la qualification foncière pour un candidat à la mairie est portée à la somme respectable de $10,000 - alors que celle du candidat à l'échevinage demeure à $2,000 - et que les exigences énumérées plus haut demeurent requises pour l'électeur. Les véritables modifications dans ce domaine appartiennent à la troisième période.

Qu'en est-il de l'émergence en force des Canadiens français sur la scène municipale? On la remarque dans la carrière de quelques maires importants à cette époque. Le premier, Jacques Grenier, est un fils de navigateur qui se lance dans les affaires à Montréal pour devenir l'un des piliers de la classe financière alors qu'il réunit quelques directorats de compagnie tout en étant le Président de la Société Saint-Jean-Baptiste. Le second, Alphonse Desjardins, pratique le droit pendant quelques années mais abandonne bientôt pour se lancer dans le journalisme, à *L'Ordre* d'abord puis comme directeur du *Nouveau-Monde*. Conservateur en politique, il siégera à Ottawa, recevra un portefeuille en 1896 pour être enfin nommé sénateur. On voit de nouveau dans cette biographie s'entremêler carrière libérale et affaires puisque Desjardins sera président du Crédit Foncier du Bas-Canada. Le troisième enfin, Raymond Préfontaine, avocat, ministre sous Laurier et surnommé le nouvel Haussmann à cause de son souci de l'aménagement urbain, occupe une place à part par le rôle qu'il a joué dans le passage de la majorité du Conseil municipal aux mains des Canadiens français.

La lecture des procès-verbaux du Conseil municipal à cette époque et des journaux devrait permettre de préciser les étapes et les stratégies de toute cette mutation.

La mesure de la transformation dans le pouvoir politique des deux principaux groupes ethniques apparaît surtout dans le Conseil municipal lui-même. Du côté des maires, la balance est parfaitement équilibrée. Dans l'ensemble des élus cependant, l'image est passablement différente. Inférieure à la moitié jusqu'en 1880, la représentation française franchit le cap du 50 pour cent au cours de cette décennie et va par la suite s'amplifier rapidement pour dépasser 73 pour cent avant la Seconde Guerre Mondiale et, de toutes façons, se maintenir aux alentours de 70 pour cent depuis le début du siècle. Un tel renversement se fait surtout au détriment du groupe écossais qui disparaîtra progressivement.

La même tendance vaut pour ce qui est de l'affiliation religieuse. Minoritaires jusqu'en 1880, les catholiques comptent 57 pour cent du groupe pendant les dix ans qui suivent et leur proportion a conservé depuis une moyenne de 75 pour cent, atteignant à certaines époques 85 pour cent.

Cette mutation allait s'accompagner de maints conflits idéologiques qu'il faudrait pouvoir examiner de près depuis 1830. Un observateur note comment, dans le dernier tiers du dix-neuvième siècle, une minorité anglo-saxonne «les Treize Nobles,» a pendant quelque temps mené le combat contre les projets de Préfontaine, l'accusant même de mener la ville au désastre. Mais cette fraction allait disparaître lentement: en votant contre des mesures qui s'avérèrent excellentes, par des dissensions internes, en changeant même de positions sur des questions fort débattues. En fin de compte, ce noyau d'opposition s'évanouit entièrement.

Pour la période qui nous occupe présentement, 1873 à 1914, cela donne un personnel politique passablement hétérogène.

La proportion des conseillers originaires de Montréal reste encore faible, environ un tiers. Pour ce qui est de leurs occupations, ils se divisent en quelques blocs de dimension à peu près égale. Un sur cinq est soit avocat, soit médecin, de profession libérale, ce qui représente une étape intermédiaire dans les progrès de cette catégorie au long des trois périodes. Ceux qui occupent de hauts postes dans l'administration sont au contraire en perte de vitesse mais leur véritable baisse ne commence qu'avec le vingtième siècle et, au cours de ces années, le quart du Conseil se retrouve dans cette couche. Leurs subalternes prennent la place. En effet, les administrateurs d'un niveau intermédiaire augmentent en flèche, surtout à compter de 1890. Dans la première décennie de ce siècle, la majorité du Conseil, soit 60 pour cent, leur appartiendra et cette position va se maintenir dans le futur quoiqu'avec peut-être un peu moins de puissance.

Une absence est remarquable dans toute cette répartition, celle des collets blancs. Jamais au cours de ces trois périodes ils n'occuperont une place importante. Leur moyenne totale atteint les 30 pour cent. On pourrait dire la même chose de ceux que l'on classe comme semi-professionnels. Il semble donc y avoir un type d'occupation qui favorise l'entrée et le succès dans la politique municipale.

La classe ouvrière n'a pas encore conquis sa place pendant ces années. Les ouvriers spécialisés et non-spécialisés sont fortement minoritaires, un peu dans la même position que les collets blancs mais avec cette différence qu'ils parviendront davantage à se tailler une zone propre après la Première Guerre. Le Conseil est pour le moment divisé entre deux groupes principaux, administrateurs et professionnels, mais on devine des forces qui vont modifier cet équilibre. Dans ce cas aussi, l'homogénéité est à peu près disparue mais les traits d'un pluralisme neuf apparaissent encore mal. L'examen du niveau d'instruction le confirmerait si nécessaire. Les catégories «secondaire» et «universitaire» augmentent pendant que le «primaire» baisse rapidement mais leurs positions respectives n'ont pas encore la stabilité que l'on peut apercevoir dans la période suivante. Il serait plus juste de parler dans ce cas-ci d'une progression encore mal assurée. Telle est l'allure d'une assemblée élue en pleine mutation comme le montrent d'ailleurs d'autres signes que nous avons déjà indiqués.

Une même diversité perce dans les carrières politiques. Pendant ces années qui font suite à la naissance du Canada, le conseiller municipal et, à plus forte raison, le maire de Montréal, est tenté par un engagement politique à un niveau plus élevé. La moitié des maires fut ainsi à un moment ou l'autre député, à Québec ou à Ottawa, et les conseillers municipaux ont à la même époque acquis l'habitude d'aller siéger au Parlement. Entre 1870 et 1879, immédiatement après la Confédération donc, quarante-six de ceux-ci sont devenus membres de l'Assemblée législative. Bien que cela constitue en fait l'objet d'une autre recherche, et déjà ces chiffres en soulignent l'intérêt, on peut dès maintenant remarquer que, de façon générale, c'est la politique provinciale qui a surtout attiré les élus municipaux, quoiqu'il arrive fréquemment qu'un même homme passe d'une capitale à l'autre.

L'allégeance partisance est moins facile à définir. Les deux grands partis ont recruté des adeptes à peu près également pendant cette période parmi les maires. Le plus célèbre est sans doute J.J.C. Abbott qui fut le troisième Premier Ministre du Canada, après la mort de Macdonald, en 1891. Il avait siégé à Québec pendant quinze ans. Au niveau des conseillers, le choix paraît plus net. Après 1867 et avant 1914, c'est le parti Libéral qui l'emporte, de manière assez tranchée dans les premières années. Mentionnons enfin une fraction de sénateurs, et beaucoup moins de conseillers législatifs, nommés surtout parmi les maires. Répétons toutefois que ces brèves remarques font ressortir beaucoup trop rapidement de lien qu'on devine fort solide entre la politique municipale montréalaise et les niveaux provincial et fédéral. Beaucoup d'autres indices seraient à considérer dans une étude complète de cette question.

Le moment est maintenant arrivé où prend fin cette période de réaménagement. Avec le vingtième siècle et la Première Guerre Mondiale apparaît une nouvelle génération d'hommes politiques montréalais.

1914-1960: Les nouveaux hommes politiques

S'il fallait parvenir à isoler l'essentiel de ce qui caractérise cette troisième période, c'est sans aucun doute à la promotion du nombre comme ressource politique que reviendrait ce prestige.

Au moment de la Première Guerre Mondiale, la population de Montréal a dépassé le demi-million et depuis un demi-siècle nul ne pourra être maire de Montréal sans recueiller l'adhésion d'une vaste fraction de cet ensemble. En même temps, se trouve consacrée la baisse de certaines autres valeurs politiques qui avaient déjà eu leur moment de gloire. Par exemple, les milieux d'affaires et de haute finance se sont plus ou moins retirés de la direction de la politique municipale, du moins de ses cadres officiels. De même, la carrière intellectuelle sera supplantée par la popularité. Et surtout, le statut social ne saurait aucunement suffire à assurer une place dans l'élite politique. Les électeurs veulent être représentés par des hommes davantage conformes au type moyen: le peuple aime se reconnaître parmi ses chefs, ce qui n'entraîne pas toutefois un quelconque nivellement dans la personnalité des leaders montréalais de cette dernière époque, bien au contraire puisque ainsi que nous le verrons, s'inscrivent ici les noms de quelques-uns des principaux leaders qu'ait connu la ville.

En bref, cette nouvelle génération d'hommes politiques confirme la disparition d'une élite unique dans la vie montréalaise. Chaque domaine de l'activité sociale a ses propres chefs qui sont de moins en moins interchangeables et l'action politique va tendre à se «professionnaliser» c'est-à-dire qu'elle va devenir l'affaire d'une catégorie d'hommes qui en font leur occupation unique. Un tableau complet des élites montréalaises, qui demeure notre but à long terme, devra maintenant tenir compte de nombreux secteurs et de groupes d'hommes passablement différenciés. Cette hypothèse générale reçoit à coup sûr une première vérification par l'examen des traits caractéristiques de ceux qui vont maintenant entrer à l'Hôtel de Ville.

A quelles causes doit-on rattacher cette profonde transformation? Deux d'entre elles possèdent un relief à part comme va le montrer l'examen attentif de ce nouveau type de leader.

La première se rapporte au système électoral lui-même. Bien sûr, le maire est élu au suffrage universel depuis 1852 et les électeurs restent divisés selon les trois grandes catégories formées en

1860. Pourtant 1910 va marquer une étape car ce moment est celui de l'abolition à peu près totale des qualifications exigées aussi bien de l'électeur que du candidat. Pour se présenter à la mairie, en 1910, il fallait posséder des biens d'une valeur de $10,000; on fera disparaître cette règle l'année suivante. Même évolution pour le candidat-échevin: depuis quarante ans on exigeait de lui un avoir d'au moins $2,000; il n'en sera plus ainsi à compter de 1912. Jusqu'en 1937, la seule exigence pour tout candidat sera de savoir «lire couramment et écrire lisiblement,» mais ceci même disparaîtra de la charte municipale cette année-là.

Quant aux électeurs, ce ne sera pas le véritable suffrage universel, du moins pour l'élection des échevins, avec la conservation d'une division triple accentuée entr'autres par le régime des trois classes de 1940, lequel donnait plus de votes aux propriétaires et permettait même à diverses associations de nommer des représentants, mais il reste tout de même que chaque Montréalais, pourvu qu'il soit propriétaire ou locataire, possède le droit de voter. Tout cela devait nécessairement faciliter une hausse de l'intérêt populaire pour la chose publique.

La seconde cause appartient à un phénomène déjà largement étudié, l'influence prépondérante du groupe canadien français. La ville continue de croître rapidement. On se souvient qu'entre 1911 et 1951 la population passe de 490,000 à plus d'un million.

La proportion des francophones va se solidifier pour former tout au long de cette période, rappelons-le au passage, un bloc remarquablement stable, car elle varie entre 60,2 pour cent vers les années '30, et 63,8 pour cent au recensement de 1951. Disons brièvement tout de suite, quitte à le revoir plus loin, que ceci laisse supposer une participation de plus en plus forte de l'élément canadien français dans la politique municipale: tous les maires sont de langue française depuis 1914 et au Conseil municipal les Canadiens français ont acquis une solide majorité.

Le portrait-type du nouveau leader comporte quatre grands signes distinctifs: (a) il a pour lui la popularité, ce qui s'exprime entr'autres dans des mandats répétés; (b) il est principalement d'origine française; (c) il est issu d'un milieu social moyen, son occupation est d'un niveau intermédiaire; (d) enfin, la politique active, à tous les niveaux, l'intéresse de plus en plus.

(a) La popularité transparaît d'abord dans le nombre de votes reçus. Une comparaison entre le nombre de suffrages recueillis par un maire avant et après 1910 en témoigne éloquemment. Alors qu'environ quarante-cinq mille citoyens ont exprimé leur choix en 1912, l'élection suivante, celle de 1914, en amène plus de soixante-quinze mille à se déranger. Cette première élection de Médéric Martin marque donc, de cette manière aussi, une étape. Le cap des cent mille votants sera franchi au moment de l'arrivée de Camilien Houde, soit en 1928. Bien sûr, la croissance démographique générale explique cette transformation mais elle ne saurait suffire. Entre 1901 et 1951 la population de Montréal a à peu près triplé. Pourtant, les suffrages exprimés passent du simple au quintuple. Puis, comment expliquer d'aussi profonds changements d'une élection à la suivante parfois? En 1938 il faut multiplier le chiffre initial par six.

Le nombre absolu des voix données au candidat vainqueur est un autre indice. Martin avait obtenu des votes de 50,000, Houde atteindra un sommet, 90,000 (1934) inégalé par ses successeurs avant 1960. Seul Monsieur Jean Drapeau fera mieux avec 130,000 voix en 1962.

Enfin, les majorités de certains maires confirment l'importance de la popularité. Aux alentours de 1900, la lutte est assez serrée et on voit au mieux certains maires quasi-doubler les voix obtenues par l'opposition. Houde de nouveau dépassera ce seuil en 1930 et Drapeau, après deux solides victoires en 1954 et 1960, remportera la plus forte majorité dans l'histoire montréalaise, soit près de dix fois plus de votes. Il est intéressant de noter que l'élection la plus contestée depuis 1945, celle de 1957, est aussi celle qui a connu la plus forte votation. La majorité de 10,000 remportée par Monsieur Sarto Fournier doit être mise à côté d'un grand total de plus de 160,000.

Un autre signe de la popularité: la fréquence des mandats. Sauf l'honorable Jean-Louis Beaudry qui avait été porté dix fois à la mairie, entre 1862 et 1885, la très grande majorité des maires de Montréal au dix-neuvième siècle n'avait obtenu qu'un seul mandat. La situation change après 1910. Martin a été maire à quatre reprises, Adhémar Raynault, trois fois pour un total de six ans, et surtout Camilien Houde qui a remporté sept victoires municipales, ce qui a fait de lui le maire le plus longtemps au pouvoir dans l'histoire montréalaise. Nous réservons une place à part à la carrière de

Monsieur Jean Drapeau car elle nous paraît, elle aussi, marquer une nouvelle étape. Examinons plutôt l'histoire de ces géants de la politique municipale que furent Houde et Raynault.

Celui-ci fut maire immédiatement avant et pendant la Seconde Guerre. Dans son cas, ni les antécédents familiaux, ni le statut social, ni le niveau d'éducation, ni la richesse n'auront été des facteurs importants. D'origine paysanne, il vient à Montréal où sa forte personnalité lui fait faire une bonne carrière dans les assurances. De famille libérale, il sera pourtant député Indépendant à l'Assemblée législative et ses préoccupations porteront avant tout sur la question nationale. Il appartient à la catégorie d'hommes politiques qui doivent leur carrière à leurs qualités de chef, à leur capacité d'entraîner le peuple.

Camilien Houde représente sans doute encore mieux l'époque. On a déjà beaucoup écrit sur la vie mouvementée de ce maire qui fut appelé «Monsieur Montréal» et dont les mandats totalisent dix-huit années de pouvoir sur la scène municipale. Pourtant ce succès n'est pas dû à son origine sociale: né dans un quartier populeux, il est de famille modeste, fils d'un meunier, et orphelin très jeune. Ses études s'arrêtent à seize ans. La carrière politique est ici particulièrement brillante et tumultueuse. Tour à tour député à Québec puis à Ottawa, battu puis porté en triomphe, le parti conservateur provincial en fit son chef en 1928 et il dirigea l'opposition à Québec pendant deux sessions. Sa succession devait être prise par Maurice Duplessis et les démêlés entre les deux hommes constituent en eux-mêmes un chapitre important de l'histoire récente du Québec. Houde se fera aussi élire comme indépendant au provincial en 1939. Au municipal, ses luttes restent quasi-légendaires et ont pris à quelques reprises, comme en 1934, l'allure d'un combat politique plus large alors qu'il défit le candidat-maire du parti Libéral provincial. La guerre entraîne un nouveau moment fort dans sa carrière: son opposition à la conscription le fait emprisonner et la population montréalaise le porte à la mairie en 1944. Il sera défait alors comme candidat du Bloc Populaire au Fédéral. Houde se retire de la vie publique en 1954, abandonnant la mairie pour des raisons de santé. On peut voir la puissance populaire de sa personne en notant qu'une foule de 75,000 personnes assiste à ses funérailles en septembre 1958.

Concluons donc cette analyse de la popularité en notant

qu'entre 1914 et 1960, quatre maires seulement totalisent trente-neuf années de pouvoir et ont amené les plus fortes proportions de votants.

(b) L'origine ethnique joue tout au long de cette période un rôle majeur. Du côté des maires, la loi de l'alternance qui avait eu cours depuis le début de l'histoire politique municipale est brisée en 1914 par l'élection de Médéric Martin qui suivit le mandat d'un autre Canadien français, Louis-Arsène Lavallée. On peut croire que l'élément français, conscient de sa force numérique, exigea alors que le chef de la ville fut choisi chez lui. Ce que confirme le fait que depuis un demi-siècle aucun maire de langue anglaise ne fut porté au pouvoir malgré quelques candidatures. Les majorités recueillies par les représentants français apportent aussi des précisions: celles de Médéric Martin sur son adversaire anglophone voisinaient les sept mille, mais en 1930 Houde doublera le nombre de voix du candidat Mathewson et après cette date aucun Canadien anglais ne fera une lutte serrée à la mairie.

Même mouvement chez les conseillers. Mise en place au siècle précédent, la majorité française au Conseil municipal s'affirme depuis 1914 puisqu'elle a constamment voisiné les 70 pour cent. Comparée au pourcentage de Canadiens français que compte la population de Montréal, cette représentation est donc un peu au-dessus d'une stricte image.

L'élément anglophone donne une représentation plus fidèle. A peu près 25 pour cent de la population montréalaise depuis 1911, il a obtenu environ 23 pour cent des sièges au Conseil municipal. On peut noter ici la disparition quasi-complète des Écossais qui, rappelons-le, avaient pourtant exercé beaucoup d'influence il y a un siècle. La même remarque vaut pour les Irlandais. Les autres groupes ethniques sont en général sous-représentés dans cette assemblée. Les Juifs qui forment entre 5 et 6 pour cent de la population montréalaise n'ont qu'une moyenne de 2 pour cent des leurs parmi les élus. Les Italiens en doublant leur proportion dans l'ensemble n'ont guère été représentés avant 1950 et, même depuis cette date, leur nombre de conseillers est inférieur d'une bonne moitié à leur place dans la population. Les Polonais sont 1 pour cent de la population en 1951 mais un seul des leurs va être élu avant 1960.

(c) Ce nouveau leader qui a pour lui le nombre et l'origine ethnique vient de façon générale d'un milieu modeste et n'a pas lui-même occupé des postes élevés dans la structure socio-économique de la ville comme l'avaient fait ceux du siècle précédent. Il y a bien eu quelques professionnels, avocats exclusivement, mais ceux-ci n'ont guère fait carrière de ce côté. Deux des plus importants se sont lancés dans la politique active avant le trentaine. Il y a eu aussi un journaliste, fils d'avocat, l'honorable Fernand Rinfret qui fut Secrétaire d'Etat sous Mackenzie King, mais le rappel que nous avons fait de la carrière des principaux maires de cette période montre assez que ces hommes ne sont pas de la même catégorie que les puissants financiers de la première période ou les universitaires renommés et les journalistes de la seconde.

De façon plus générale, l'ensemble des conseillers élus depuis cinquante ans témoigne de l'accession au pouvoir de la classe moyenne. En effet, si la proportion de ceux qui n'ont que des études primaires a eu tendance à baisser, celle de ceux qui ont profité d'une formation universitaire a augmenté considérablement l'emportant ainsi sur les titulaires d'un diplôme secondaire qui avaient formé jusqu'en 1950 un bloc d'environ 20 pour cent pour être coupé du tiers après cette date.

Un examen des occupations permet de préciser cette émergence de la classe moyenne. Les professionnels forment entre le cinquième et le quart des élus actuellement, ce qui ne s'éloigne pas tellement d'une tendance valable pour les cent vingt dernières années. Mais les gérants et hauts administrateurs ont accusé une baisse significative, particulièrement depuis le tournant du siècle: d'une moyenne de 33 pour cent, à la première période, ils passent à une fraction d'environ 10 pour cent. Le profit de cette mutation ira aux petits administrateurs (agents d'assurances, commis, marchands, etc.) et à la classe ouvrière. Les premiers en viendront à fournir quasi la moitié du Conseil municipal après 1900 tandis que les ouvriers en forment le dixième, ce qui est à peu près le double de leurs effectifs antérieurs.

(d) Dernière caractéristique, le nouveau leader montréalais, dans le prolongement d'un engagement amorcé depuis 1867, prend une part très active à la vie politique provinciale et fédérale. Sur les sept derniers maires de Montréal, six se sont lancés, à un moment ou l'autre, dans le combat partisan: l'un est devenu ministre; un autre chef d'un parti provincial; un troisième a été nommé sénateur; un autre, conseiller législatif; enfin cinq ont été députés. Comme on l'a vu, l'un de ces maires, Houde, a eu une influence politique considérable sur le plan provincial et se dessine ici aussi une tendance qui paraît devoir s'affirmer de plus en plus nettement.

C'est ce dont témoignent aussi les affiliations politiques des conseillers municipaux. Une vingtaine de ceux-ci à chaque élection ont été ou sont devenus membres du parlement québecois, ce qui représente une certaine baisse par rapport aux deux décennies qui ont suivi la Confédération mais montre aussi une stabilisation indiscutable dans le nombre de ceux qui entendent mener une carrière politique à divers niveaux. Signalons encore que le Parlement fédéral semble être moins recherché par les conseillers. Le parti Libéral jouit chez ceux-ci d'une plus grande faveur, ce qui n'est guère étonnant quand on songe aux pourcentages du vote que ce parti recueille actuellement dans la région montréalaise.

Vers un nouveau type de leader municipal?

Peut-on prévoir quel type de leader Montréal va dégager dans les années à venir? Très difficilement parce qu'une nouvelle coupure, si elle existe, serait tout-à-fait récente. Vouloir la situer après la Seconde Guerre paraît erroné car pendant près de dix ans encore la politique municipale sera dominée par Houde dont nous avons fait en quelque sorte le prototype de la troisième période. La démarcation daterait donc de 1955, ce qui constitue une période bien courte, dans les années que nous avons considérées, pour asseoir une prévision valable. Pourtant, il faut risquer cette hypothèse un peu générale selon laquelle le leadership montréalais subit actuellement une transformation profonde.

Divers signes nous invitent tout au moins à le faire sous réserve d'un examen plus approfondi quand le temps aura passé. D'abord, Montréal est sorti depuis quelques années d'une phase de dépendance marquée surtout par les tutelles de 1918 à 1921 et de 1940 à 1944. On admet en général que la ville connaît depuis 1945 une phase d'expansion remarquable, tant sur le plan économique que démographique. Ne constitue-t-elle pas présentement plus de 40 pour cent de la population de toute la Province de Québec? Les fonctions nouvelles que la ville remplit, les multiples entreprises, parfois gigantesques, dont elle est le siège, tout cela laisse croire que son administration va exiger dans les années à venir des hommes munis sûrement des ressources politiques que nous avons déjà mentionnées: popularité, nombre, origine ethnique, mais aussi armés des attributs de la compétence et de la capacité administrative. Montréal est en train de connaître l'entrée en scène des experts. La technocratie ici aussi conquiert ses droits de cité. Est-ce une pure coïncidence si date de 1960, année terminale de notre étude, une vaste enquête sur l'administration municipale, confiée à une maison de spécialistes?

D'autre part, la carrière même du maire actuel de Montréal vient appuyer notre affirmation. Monsieur Jean Drapeau participe au type de leader que nous venons d'esquisser, il a pour lui la popularité. A la mairie d'abord entre 1954 et 1957, il l'occupe de nouveau depuis 1960 ce qui le place déjà aux tout premiers rangs des maires les plus longtemps au pouvoir. Avocat, sa carrière politique extra-municipale est importante. Ce qui frappe est son choix depuis une dizaine d'années du champ politique municipal auquel il a donné une orientation profondément neuve. Mentionnons seulement la relance de la politique d'annexion depuis 1960 et ces deux énormes entreprises que sont la construction d'un métro et l'organisation de l'Exposition Universelle de 1967.

Pour mener à bonne fin une telle expansion une puissante administration devient indispensable. En bref, répétons-le, la carrière politique municipale se «professionnalise,» ce qu'elle avait commencé de faire avant 1955, mais elle le poursuit d'une manière encore plus nette depuis. Il y aura par exemple une étude intéressante à mener sur la division du travail dans l'équipe dirigeante à Montréal entre les fonctions représentatives et les fonctions administratives. Les rôles sont plus clairement définis.

De tout cela on peut déjà prévoir les répercussions sur la politique provinciale tout au moins. Ceux qui dirigeront une communauté aussi vaste et aussi puissante seront de plus en plus en mesure de peser sur l'orientation du Québec et de plusieurs manières. Peut-être aussi trouveront-ils là le lien d'un apprentissage qui facilitera ensuite le passage à un autre niveau de la vie politique de notre société. Ces quelques aspects encore très imprécis et dont les réponses sont encore plus mal formulées suffisent à faire voir qu'une évolution est en cours et que notre étude se devait de la mentionner.

Il ne saurait être question de conclure, du moins de façon définitive, une telle analyse. On voit trop souvent que l'explication finale en bien des cas appelle plusieurs approfondissements sur des points précis pour oser affirmer que les lignes de force de l'évolution du personnel politique montréalais sont entièrement et clairement connues. Notre analyse a d'abord voulu indiquer les regroupements que suggère une connaissance fouillée des élus municipaux. Statistiques à l'appui, sans pour autant les laisser alourdir ce texte, des configurations ont pu être dessinées. Mais il est évident que cette phase n'explique pas tout par elle-même.

A plusieurs reprises, la mise en relation des divers aspects de cette compilation a suggéré des hypothèses que d'autres démarches, rappel historique, comparaisons dans le temps, ont confirmé. L'homme politique montréalais a ainsi été circonscrit. On peut maintenant en établir, selon les moments, le portrait-type. Mais en même temps on ne peut s'empêcher de souhaiter que des études différentes et variées, sur l'histoire générale du Québec, son évolution socio-économique, viennent ou bien préciser les résultats atteints à ce niveau, ou bien, et peut-être davantage, ajouter des éléments nouveaux à la réponse de la question que nous indiquions au tout début: qui gouverne à Montréal? La structure institutionnelle et le processus réel du pouvoir paraissent être, dans cette optique, deux voies particulièrement prometteuses. Entre ces divers aspects d'un même phénomène une certaine pondération pourra alors être définie.

En tout cas, il semble maintenant indiscutable que toute étude sur la vie politique montréalaise met en cause et fait surgir plusieurs des problèmes et traits fondamentaux de la société canadienne française et canadienne.

Vancouver Civic Party Leadership: Backgrounds, Attitudes and Non-Civic Party Affiliations

ROBERT EASTON and PAUL TENNANT

During 1968 there was more political activity in Vancouver than at any other time in recent decades. Two new political parties, The Electors Action Movement (TEAM) and the Committee of Progressive Electors (COPE), were formed to challenge the Civic Non-Partisan Association (NPA), which had dominated Vancouver politics since the early 1940's. TEAM was created in the early months of the year and by the December election had 963 paid-up members; COPE was formed later in the year and grew to include several hundred members. In the December election the NPA remained dominant, electing the mayor and a majority of aldermen, school trustees, and Parks Board members; TEAM elected two aldermen, three school trustees, and one Parks Board member; COPE elected only the incumbent alderman who had been its chief organizer. It was evident to observers that the NPA was led by anti-socialist businessmen and lawyers who, in their non-civic political roles, were supporters of the Social Credit, Liberal, or Conservative parties. From the time the TEAM organization was formed conflicting observations and interpretations about it were made by journalists and even by TEAM leaders themselves. Impressions of COPE were influenced primarily by what was known of the alderman who founded the organization, and thus, like him, it was considered to be oriented towards socialism, unionism, and the interests of the working class sections of the city.

Completely lacking for all three parties, however, were explanations based on extensive studies of the influential members of the

From *B. C. Studies*, Summer, 1969. pp. 19-29. Reprinted by permission.

parties. For this reason, shortly after the 1968 election, members of the Urban Politics Research Seminar at the University of British Columbia designed a written questionnaire to obtain information on the backgrounds, attitudes, and provincial and national political affiliations of party leaders. Leaders were defined as those who had held formal positions within the party organization (including the position of candidate for public office) and those who had not held such positions but were considered influential by knowledgeable members of their parties. In April and May of 1969 the questionnaire was taken in person by one of the authors to each of the leaders who could be reached. The questionnaire was completed by 30 NPA leaders, 45 TEAM leaders, and 27 COPE leaders. The response rate was approximately 80 per cent among those who were reached and approximately 67 per cent among those originally identified as party leaders. The majority of those who were not reached had played, compared to other leaders, a minor part in their parties.

No attempt is made here to compare the characteristics of the respondents with those of the Vancouver population, although in the case of social characteristics this could easily be done using census data. The percentage tables themselves need little explanation – Table 3, for example, shows that every leader reached responded to the question dealing with education, and that 73.3 per cent of the 45 TEAM respondents were university graduates. Because of the rounding of percentage figures to the nearest one-tenth per cent, the percentage columns do not always add up to exactly 100 per cent. The "all parties" columns give the characteristics of the respondents as a single group without regard to party affiliation. The "NPA," "TEAM," and "COPE" columns indicate something of the gross differences between the three groups of leaders. Table 4, for example, shows that the NPA group has higher incomes than those of the TEAM and COPE groups, although it does not give information about average incomes or the range of incomes. The differences *within* each group are especially interesting. Still using Table 4 as an example, one sees that NPA responses are skewed towards one end of the scale, that COPE responses are skewed towards the opposite end, and that TEAM responses, quite unlike those of the other two groups, are concentrated in the middle of the scale. Moreover, TEAM's "end" responses fall, in terms of magnitude, between the end responses of the other two groups. In other words, there is an NPA-COPE polarization, with TEAM occupying a middle position. Should this pattern recur in a number of scales one may conclude not only that there are fundamental differences between the three parties, but also that the Vancouver party system forms a continuum in which the NPA occupies one end, TEAM the middle, and COPE the other end. These conclusions are inescapable in the present study. The fact of the continuum, however, is less noteworthy than the large degree and wide range of the differences between the three parties.

Social Composition of NPA, TEAM, and COPE Leadership

The tables in this section deal with the variables of occupation, occupational status, education, income, age, religion, numbers of their civic organizations to which respondents belong, and self-perceptions of membership in a social class. Each table reveals significant differences between the three groups. Two other social variables, those of sex and of length of residence in Vancouver, were examined, but the distribution for each was found to be generally similar in each party. Women respondents constituted 10 per cent of the total in the NPA; 22 per cent in TEAM; and 15 per cent in COPE. Proportions of respondents in each group who had lived in Vancouver for less than fifteen years were 10 per cent in the NPA; 25 per cent in TEAM; and 12 per cent in COPE. The occupational classifications and their status rankings used in Table 1 are those which have been presented by Peter C. Pineo and John Porter, with the exception of the "union officials" and "housewives" categories which, because of their importance in the present case, have been added and arbitrarily assigned the status ranking shown.[1] As one compares Tables 4 and 5, the question of whether the differences in income distribution are related more to age than to party might be raised. Such is not the case, however, for a direct comparison of age and income showed that among the respondents the two factors were unrelated.

Ideology and Outlook of NPA, TEAM, and COPE Leadership

To assess the ideology and outlook of respondents, four sets of

[1] Peter C. Pineo and John Porter, "Occupational prestige in Canada," *Canadian Review of Sociology and Anthropology*, IV (February, 1947), pp. 41-53.

Table 1. Occupations and Civic Party

		NPA	TEAM	COPE	ALL PARTIES
1	Lawyers	20.1	13.1	4.8	13.5
	School Teachers	3.3	10.7	19.0	10.1
	University Professors	—	13.1	—	5.6
	Engineers, Dentists, Accountants	—	2.6	9.5	3.4
	(Total Professional)	(23.4)	(39.5)	(33.3)	(32.6)
2	Proprietors, managers, and officials of large firms	50.0	15.8	—	23.6
3	Semi-professionals (social workers, brokers, librarians, clergymen)	—	18.4	—	7.9
4	Proprietors, managers, and officials of small firms	23.4	5.3	—	10.1
5	Union Officials	—	2.6	23.8	6.7
6	Clerical and Sales persons	—	5.3	4.8	3.4
7	Housewives	3.3	13.1	14.3	10.1
8	Skilled and unskilled labourers	—	—	23.8	5.6
N	(number of respondents to question)	30	38	21	89

Note: In this and the following tables, all figures are expressed as percentages, except those in the "N" columns which are totals.

Table 2. Occupational Status and Civic Party (based on Table 1)

	Low (6, 7, 8)	Medium (3, 4, 5)	High (1, 2)	N
NPA	3.3	23.4	73.4	30
TEAM	18.4	26.3	55.3	38
COPE	42.9	23.8	33.3	21
ALL PARTIES	19.1	24.7	56.2	89

Table 3. Education and Civic Party

	High school graduation or less	Some University	University Graduation	N
NPA	26.7	26.7	46.7	30
TEAM	11.1	15.6	73.3	45
COPE	55.6	18.5	25.9	27
ALL PARTIES	27.5	19.6	52.9	102

Table 4. Annual Income and Civic Party

	−$7500	$7500-$15,000	+$15,000	N
NPA	10.7	28.6	60.7	28
TEAM	13.9	52.8	33.3	36
COPE	50.0	45.0	5.0	20
ALL PARTIES	21.4	42.9	35.7	84

Table 5. Age and Civic Party

	−40 yrs.	40-50 yrs.	+50 yrs.	N
NPA	23.3	23.3	53.3	30
TEAM	53.3	26.7	20.0	45
COPE	38.5	23.1	38.5	26
ALL PARTIES	40.6	24.8	34.6	101

Table 6. Religious Preference and Civic Party

	Catholic	Protestant	Jewish	None	N
NPA	10.3	75.9	—	13.8	29
TEAM	2.5	47.5	10.0	39.5	40
COPE	3.7	7.4	—	88.9	27
ALL PARTIES	5.2	44.8	4.2	45.8	96

Table 7. Membership in Other Civic Organizations

	0, 1, 2,	3 or 4	5+	N
NPA	10.3	20.7	69.0	29
TEAM	31.0	38.1	31.0	42
COPE	46.2	34.6	19.2	26
ALL PARTIES	28.9	32.0	39.2	97

Table 8. Social Class and Civic Party (Self-Perception of Respondents)

	Working or lower middle	Middle Class	Upper Class	N
NPA	11.1	77.8	11.1	27
TEAM	10.8	75.7	13.5	37
COPE	66.7	33.3	—	24
ALL PARTIES	26.1	64.8	9.1	88

questions were asked relating to the attitudinal dimensions of "individualism-collectivism," "traditionalism-progressivism," "élitism-democracy," and "pessimism-optimism." "Individualism" was treated in the classical Manchester liberal sense; "traditionalism" in the Oakeshottian sense of valuing what has been achieved; "élitism," in the sense of believing that only a minority are suited to govern; and "optimism," in the sense of believing that man is capable of triumphing over his basic problems. From the responses to the sets of questions the following Tables 9 to 12 were derived.[2] Without exception, on these basic political variables there is a polarization between the NPA and COPE, while TEAM responses are more evenly distributed, with the highest proportion of responses in the "moderate" category. Clearly, despite the predilection of social scientists to consider ideology dead, it is alive and thriving in Vancouver.

Positions of NPA, TEAM, and COPE Leadership on Vancouver Political Issues

Among the issues in the 1968 Vancouver election campaign were two which, although usually discussed only obliquely by the contestants, may be considered basic to Vancouver city politics. One of

[2] Although the sets of questions and the procedures used in deriving the scales are not presented in this article, they may be obtained by writing to the authors.

Table 9. Attitudes on Individualism-Collectivism Dimension

	Individualist	Moderate	Collectivist	N
NPA	76.7	16.7	6.7	30
TEAM	28.9	46.7	24.4	45
COPE	—	18.5	81.5	27
ALL PARTIES	35.3	30.4	34.3	102

Table 10. Attitudes on Traditionalism-Progressivism Dimension

	Traditionalist	Moderate	Progressive	N
NPA	56.7	23.3	20.0	30
TEAM	26.7	40.0	33.3	45
COPE	3.7	18.5	77.8	27
ALL PARTIES	29.4	29.4	41.2	102

Table 11. Attitudes on Élitism-Democracy Dimension

	Élitist	Moderate	Democratic	N
NPA	46.7	46.7	6.7	30
TEAM	17.8	66.7	15.6	45
COPE	3.7	33.3	63.0	27
ALL PARTIES	22.5	52.0	25.5	102

Table 12. Attitudes on Pessimism-Optimism Dimension

	Pessimist	Optimist	N
NPA	73.3	26.7	30
TEAM	55.6	44.4	45
COPE	33.3	66.7	27
ALL PARTIES	54.9	45.1	102

these is whether the institutions of civic politics encourage democracy, or, on the contrary, élitism; the other is whether national and provincial political parties should compete in civic elections. Another issue, like these two related to what might be termed the form of political regime, but unlike them an explicit issue in the 1968 campaign, was whether Vancouver should return to the ward system (which had been abolished in the mid-1930's). TEAM and COPE favoured the return; the NPA did not. Among the various issues having to do with government action rather than form of government was whether the city should provide children's day-care centres. TEAM and COPE advocated such centres; the NPA candidates did not. There were other issues in the campaign, but these four are sufficient to provide further insight into the nature of the NPA, TEAM, and COPE.

For each of four statements (given as the titles of the following tables) the respondents were asked to give their position on a seven point Likert scale: (1) strongly agree, (2) moderately agree, (3) slightly agree, (4) uncertain, (5) slightly disagree, (6) moderately disagree, (7) strongly disagree. In the tables the numbers heading the vertical columns indicate which of the seven categories have been combined to form the three-point scales. As is evident, the NPA-COPE polarization continues, with TEAM responses in each case more evenly distributed.

Table 13. Vancouver Civic Institutions Do Not Encourage Democracy

	1,2	3,4,5	6,7	N
NPA	13.3	16.7	70.0	30
TEAM	46.7	35.6	17.8	45
COPE	70.4	22.2	7.4	27
ALL PARTIES	43.1	26.5	30.4	102

Table 14. It Would Be Dangerous if National Political Parties Also Competed at the Civic Level

	1,2	3,4,5	6,7	N
NPA	76.7	16.7	6.7	30
TEAM	35.6	35.6	28.9	45
COPE	4.0	16.0	80.0	25
ALL PARTIES	40.0	25.0	35.0	100

Non-Civic Political Roles of NPA, TEAM, and COPE Leadership

To an outsider the question of non-civic political activities and preferences of those who are active in Vancouver civic politics may

Table 15. Vancouver Should Have a Ward System

	1	2,3	4,5,6,7	N
NPA	—	13.3	86.7	30
TEAM	40.0	37.8	22.2	45
COPE	85.2	14.8	—	27
ALL PARTIES	40.2	24.5	35.3	102

Table 16. The City Government Should Provide Day-Care Centres for Children

	1	2,3	4,5,6,7	N
NPA	13.3	23.3	63.3	30
TEAM	31.1	51.1	17.8	45
COPE	85.2	14.8	—	27
ALL PARTIES	40.2	33.3	26.5	102

appear insignificant and uninteresting, either because the outsider may assume that civic party organizations are simply aspects of party organizations also active at other levels (as they often are in America and Great Britain), or because the question is irrelevant, given the fact that provincial and national parties do not normally contest Vancouver civic elections. In reality, however, the question of provincial and national party preferences is of obsessive interest to those who are active in civic politics. As has been indicated, observers were aware that the NPA consisted of supporters of the non-socialist parties and that COPE was evidently composed chiefly of New Democratic party supporters. The case of TEAM was less clear-cut. Its founders were mostly Liberals, but they were soon joined by prominent Conservatives; TEAM contained some prominent New Democrats, yet it also contained at least some erstwhile supporters of the NPA (two of them incumbent aldermen, both of whom returned to the NPA and were re-elected). Tables 17 and 18 provide information on the provincial and national parties supported by the respondents. To facilitate comparison Social Credit and Conservative responses have been combined, since provincial Social Credit supporters and national Conservative supporters were almost entirely the same group of persons.

The NPA is a combination of Social Creditors and Conservatives on the one hand, and of Liberals on the other. TEAM is largely Liberal nationally, but much less so provincially, at which level some Liber-

Table 17. Provincial Party Support and Civic Party

	Socred-Cons.	Lib.	N.D.P.	Other-None	N
NPA	42.9	42.9	3.6	10.7	28
TEAM	8.9	44.4	22.2	24.4	45
COPE	—	3.7	66.7	29.6	27
ALL CIVIC PARTIES	16.0	33.0	29.0	22.0	100

Table 18. National Party Support and Civic Party Membership

	Socred-Cons.	Lib.	N.D.P.	Other-None	N
NPA	35.7	50.0	3.6	10.7	28
TEAM	6.7	62.2	15.6	15.6	45
COPE	—	3.7	66.7	29.6	27
ALL CIVIC PARTIES	13.0	43.0	26.0	18.0	100

als evidently switch either to the New Democrats or to inaction. COPE is composed chiefly of New Democratic supporters but has a significant proportion of persons who support no provincial or national party. Questions thus arise about the similarities and differences between NPA Liberals and TEAM Liberals, between TEAM Liberals and TEAM New Democrats, and between TEAM New Democrats and COPE New Democrats. Reaching conclusions on these questions is made difficult by the limited numbers of respondents involved – among provincial party supporters (the category used in this analysis) there are a total of 60 Liberals and New Democrats, with the number of each group in each civic party ranging from 10 to 20.

Table 19. Position on Individualism-Collectivism Dimension[3]

	NPA Lib. (m=2)	TEAM Lib. (m=4)	TEAM New Dem. (m=7)	COPE New Dem. (m=7)	ALL CIVIC PARTIES
Individualist	100.0	90.0	20.0	11.1	56.7
Collectivist	–	10.0	80.0	88.9	43.4
N	12	20	10	18	60

[3] Responses for each group on a seven-point Likert scale were divided so as to form the two most discrete groupings. To avoid misinterpretations, in this table and the following ones the median (m) score on the seven-point scale is indicated for each group.

Nevertheless, the sharp differences revealed suggest that the conclusions may be accepted with some confidence.

The nature of the differences between Liberals and New Democrats is most clearly evident on the "individualism-collectivism" dimension.

The New Democrats, whether in TEAM or COPE, are strongly collectivist, with the median scores falling in the category representing the strongest possible collectivist attitude. The NPA and TEAM Liberals differ from one another, as their "m" scores show, but they are closer to each other than the TEAM Liberals are to the TEAM New Democrats. On the basis of this dimension, the co-operation of Liberals and New Democrats in TEAM seems strange. However, the "individualism-collectivism" dimension as it has been defined in this study related primarily to only one form of individualism: the economic form. It does not, for example, concern individualism in the intellectual sphere. If attitude towards censorship is taken as an indicator of position on intellectual individualism, then the Liberal-New Democratic division in TEAM becomes much less in magnitude, and significant divisions appear between NPA Liberals and TEAM Liberals and between TEAM New Democrats and COPE New Democrats. In addition, on this dimension of intellectual individualism, NPA members are seen to be the most collectivist and COPE members are the most individualistic.

Table 20. There Should Be No Censorship

	NPA Lib. (m=5)	TEAM Lib. (m=3)	TEAM New Dem. (m=2)	COPE New Dem. (m=1)	ALL CIVIC PARTIES
Agree most	33.3	45.0	60.0	76.5	54.2
Agree least	66.7	55.0	40.0	23.5	45.8
N	12	20	9	18	59

On the dimension of "traditionalism-progressivism," there are differences between TEAM Liberals and TEAM New Democrats, although there are also differences between TEAM and COPE New Democrats in response distribution and between TEAM and NPA Liberals in both response distribution and "m" score of responses.

Table 21. Position on Traditionalism-Progressivism Dimension

	NPA Lib. (m=4)	TEAM Lib. (m=5)	TEAM New Dem. (m=6)	COPE New Dem. (m=6)	ALL CIVIC PARTIES
Traditionalist	83.3	65.0	40.0	22.2	51.6
Progressive	16.7	35.0	60.0	77.8	48.3
N	12	20	10	18	60

Nevertheless, on two questions which relate to the "traditionalism progressivism" dimension, but which were asked separately from the set of questions on which the scales in Tables 10 and 21 are based, TEAM Liberals and TEAM New Democrats are more similar to one another than is at least one of the groups to its counterpart in the other civic party.

Table 22. The Water Supply Should Be Fluoridated[4]

	NPA Lib. (m=1)	TEAM Lib. (m=1)	TEAM New Dem. (m=1)	COPE New Dem. (m=1)	ALL CIVIC PARTIES
Agree most	66.7	75.0	70.0	55.6	66.7
Agree least	33.3	25.0	30.0	44.4	33.3
N	12	20	10	18	60

Table 23. Vancouver Should Be Working Towards Some Form of Regional Government

	NPA Lib. (m=1)	TEAM Lib. (m=1)	TEAM New Dem. (m=1)	COPE New Dem. (m=2)	ALL CIVIC PARTIES
Agree most	63.6	75.0	90.0	38.9	64.4
Agree least	36.4	25.0	10.0	61.1	35.6
N	11	20	10	18	59

Both fluoridation and regional government were major issues in Vancouver in 1968 and thus may well be related to the decision of some New Democrats to support TEAM and of other New Democrats to support COPE. Furthermore, neither fluoridation nor region-

[4]Admittedly the issue of fluoridation is one which probably relates as well to dimensions other than "traditionalism-progressivism."

al government are explicitly economic issues, and thus the suggestion is reinforced that TEAM and COPE New Democrats are in agreement mainly on economic issues and not necessarily on civic issues having no direct economic implication.

In addition there are the obvious explanations, requiring no social science survey, that TEAM New Democrats were willing to work with members of other parties at the civic level and unwilling to have the New Democratic party as such compete at the civic level, that COPE New Democrats were unwilling to work with members of other parties at the civic level, and that NPA Liberals had had an opportunity to develop loyalty to the NPA and may have been unwilling to work with socialists at the civic level. (The first interpretation is supported by the fact, not widely known, of the unsuccessful behind-the-scenes effort of the TEAM executive to persuade the founder of COPE to have his group coalesce with TEAM.)

Finally two social variables seem to divide TEAM New Democrats from COPE New Democrats and to unite TEAM Liberals and TEAM New Democrats. First, 61 per cent of COPE New Democrats, but only 20 per cent of TEAM New Democrats, perceive themselves to be in the working class. This observation is of importance, for it has been well documented that members of the working class are much more likely to be liberal in economic than in non-economic issues.[5] Secondly, as far as amount of education is concerned there are close similarities between TEAM Liberals and TEAM New Democrats, sharp differences between TEAM and COPE New Democrats, and significant differences between TEAM and NPA Liberals.

Table 24. Amount of Education

	NPA Lib.	TEAM Lib.	TEAM New Dem.	COPE New Dem.	ALL CIVIC PARTIES
University Graduation	50.0	65.0	70.0	27.8	51.7
Less than University Graduation	50.0	35.0	30.0	72.2	48.3
N	12	20	10	18	60

[5] See, for example, Seymour Martin Lipset, *Political Man* (Garden City: Anchor Books, 1963), pp. 87-126.

Conclusion

It is clear that the leaderships of the Civic Non-Partisan Association, The Electors Action Movement, and the Committee of Progressive Electors are distinct from one another in social composition, ideology, and outlook, positions on contemporary civic issues, and support of national and provincial political parties. It may be suggested as well that New Democratic party supporters in TEAM are distinct from New Democratic supporters in COPE in terms of social make-up, ideology and outlook on economic issues, and positions on contemporary civic issues. Liberal supporters in the NPA would seem to be distinct from Liberal supporters in TEAM primarily in terms of existing loyalties and attitudes towards co-operating with socialists at the civic level.

The Institutional and Role Perceptions of Local Aldermen

ALAN ALEXANDER

On January 1, 1970, the cities of Port Arthur and Fort William, in Northwestern Ontario, were amalgamated to form the new city of Thunder Bay. The cities had been incorporated within a year of each other in 1906-1907 and although they existed in a single urban area and were fully contiguous a deep local rivalry and separate senses of community identity had been present for most of their history.[1] Superficially also, the functioning of civic government presented striking contrasts in institutional structure, decision-making processes and administrative efficiency.

The research upon which this study is based was conducted during the winter of 1968-1969. All members of the council of Port Arthur were interviewed, as were seven of the twelve Fort William aldermen. The method employed was to interview members of the councils intensively. The interviews were based on an open-ended questionnaire and the conversations were recorded on tape and then transcribed verbatim. The questions asked ranged from specific enquiries regarding the respondent's perceptions of his own role in the government of his community ("How do you view your job as an alderman?"), through his perceptions of the importance of issues and the influence of individuals on the workings of council, to perceptions of the position of municipal government *vis-à-vis* the

A slightly revised version of a paper presented to the Forty-Second Annual Meeting of the Canadian Political Science Association, University of Manitoba, Winnipeg, June 1970. Reprinted by permission of *The Lakehead University Review*, 1972, Vol. v, No. 1.

[1] See, Elizabeth Arthur, "The Landing and the Plot," *Lakehead University Review*, 1 (Spring, 1968), pp. 1-17.

other levels of government. This paper attempts to analyse the perceptions which aldermen had of their relationship with the community and the electorate. Some preliminary analysis of influence patterns is also included.[2]

The most striking finding to emerge from the research was the picture of the degree to which aldermen's perceptions of their own role varied and were ill-defined. In both cities the most common responses were that being elected to council was a method of self-fulfilment or self-satisfaction, that it gave evidence of "a sense of responsibility" or was a species of self-assertion. Also, the board of directors analogy was mentioned frequently, with the city likened to a business corporation and the council to its board. This conception seemed to underlie the responses of most of the aldermen, and their conversations seemed to suggest that their constituents were primarily tax-payers whose communal assets were under the management of the council. These notions of responsibility to the community and the related brokerage function of the council were not pursued to the point where aldermen took care to be responsive to articulated demands from their constituents. No alderman felt that it was necessary to establish any formal communication link with his constituents between elections and none seemed to go further in the assessment of public opinion on important (important, that is, in the perception of the alderman himself) issues than informal and chance contact with individuals in his own professional and social group.

The significance of the process of communication between the rulers and the ruled is closely related to the necessity of articulating citizen demands and translating them into political actions. Although it is usual for this process to be organized by such institutions as political parties, the kind of informality of communication described above could produce an effective demands-action continuum, but only if the elected body (the council) were seen to be broadly representative of the social, occupational, and educational composition of the community. It is unlikely that such representativeness will be achieved through the completely haphazard and random methods whereby individuals are recruited for office at the municipal level. The word "haphazard" is used in this context to

[2]This analysis will be expanded in a further paper to be entitled "Conflict, Consensus, and Decision-Making in Two Small Urban Councils."

indicate that there exists no formal organization in the community which has as one of its functions the recruitment of candidates for public office at the municipal level. The political parties in the area had, up until the time that this research was conducted, taken no official part in municipal politics.[3] Thus the "articulation of demands" function performed by parties in relation to other political institutions was lacking, although, as will be shown later, there was some partisan identification among councillors.

Table 1 demonstrates the comparison between the educational level of councillors and the educational level of the electorate at large.[4] It is obvious that the educational level of the council members is substantially higher than that of the community at large and it is particularly significant that over half of those members who agreed to be interviewed had had formal education beyond high school. It is possible to argue tentatively from these figures that people with a higher level of formal education are likely to be more highly motivated towards public service and, from the practical point of view, are likely to be engaged in occupations which facilitate membership on council by making available the time necessary to service on the council and its committees. Indeed, this conclusion is supported by research on local councillors and community influ-

Table 1. Educational Level of Electorate and Councillors

Education Ended	Electorate*	Councillors
Grades 1-5	4.3%	—
Grades 6-9	25.8%	23.5%
Grades 10-13	58.5%	23.5%
Beyond Grade 13	11.2%	53.0%

* Source: Davies survey 1968.

[3] In the election campaign for the first council of the new City of Thunder Bay, the New Democratic Party contested several council seats and the mayoralty. No other political party ran candidates and no NDP candidate was elected.

[4] For statistics on the social, educational, and occupational composition of the electorate, I am indebted to Professor Ivor G. Davies of the Department of Geography, Lakehead University. The survey from which the figures are drawn was a 2 per cent systematic sample of households based upon a randomly selected starting point. The survey was conducted in Autumn, 1968.

Table 2. Occupational Classification of Electorate and Councillors

Occupational Type	Electorate*	Councillors
Professional	11.5%	41.0
Managerial	5.4%	35.3%
Clerical	23.8%	5.9%
Skilled Manual	12.9%	—
Semi-Skilled Manual	5.4%	5.9%
Unskilled	31.2%	—
Retired	7.5%	11.8%

* Source: Davies survey 1968.

entials which has been conducted in the United Kingdom and the United States.[5]

When the same sort of comparison is made between the occupations of members of the community and the council, the latter is seen to be even less representative of the community. This is shown in Table 2.

These statistics, together with the data collected by interview, demonstrate that the degree to which the council is representative of the social, educational and occupational composition of the community is not such that meaningful feedback from the ruled to the rulers is possible, except at elections. The communications between elections are at best informal and at worst non-existent. Other data collected demonstrated that councillors were overwhelmingly antipathetic to the introduction of any devices into the municipal arena which would interfere with their freedom to decide upon issues in light of their individual view of what was best for the community and of what the electorate wanted.[6] Two possible methods of providing councillors with better articulated and more accurate infor-

[5] See, for example, G. Belknap and R. Smuckler, "Political Power Relations in a Mid-West City," *Public Opinion Quarterly*, 20 (1956), pp. 72-81; L. J. Sharpe, "Elected Representatives in Local Government," *British Journal of Sociology*, 13 (1962), pp. 189-208; F. A. Stewart, "A Sociometric Study of Influence in Southtown," *Sociometry*, 10 (1947), pp. 11-31.

[6] Some of the misperceptions which may arise from this kind of informality of communication are discussed in R. S. Sigel and H. P. Friesema, "Urban Community Leaders' Knowledge of Public Opinion," *Western Political Quarterly*, 18 (1965), pp. 881-895.

mation on the desires of the community were suggested: 1) the introduction of party politics and, 2) the use of referenda and plebiscites.

On the question of party politics, only one respondent was in favour of running municipal elections on partisan lines. Those who were opposed to the introduction of party politics, moreover, were often violently so and phrases like "political parties interfere too much," "I want to remain my own man," "There should be nothing that is going to interfere with his (the alderman's) judgment" were common in the responses. Also, there was, underlying the conversations on this point, a fairly general conviction that political parties as institutions have an independent existence unrelated to the functions of representation. No respondent displayed any awareness that parties might exist as a channel of communication between the rulers and ruled and their perceptions of political parties were overwhelmingly sinister and maleficent. Paradoxically, however, many respondents qualified their remarks by saying that they found party politics quite acceptable and indeed necessary at the higher levels of government.

In response to a question on the use of referenda and plebiscites on local issues, well over half of the respondents indicated that they were totally opposed to the idea of this kind of popular involvement, while the remainder felt that only "important" issues would be handled in this way. The criteria of "importance" were, however, very personal and subjective and the examples given were not of general areas but of specific issues. One alderman, for example, felt that the question of fluoride in the water supply should always be placed before the electorate since this was the only way to ensure that fluoridation would not be implemented.[7] Among those who were opposed, in principle, to the use of plebiscites and referenda there was a higher degree of sophistication in the arguments than was found in the opinions on party politics. In general, it was felt that plebiscites were contradictory to the principle of representative government and the arguments against their use typically referred to

[7] Evidence from the United States, however, indicates that this remark may have been based more on knowledge of the Council than of the electorate. Statistics in R. L. Crain, *et al.*, *The Politics of Community Conflict* (Indianapolis, 1969), show that whereas the adoption rate for fluoridation in forty-eight states was 32.1 per cent, the success rate in referenda was 41 per cent.

the right of the electorate to refuse to re-elect aldermen if it opposed decisions taken by them. In common with the responses on party politics, however, there was an obvious distaste for any process which might interfere with the aldermen's free exercise of judgment.

During the interviews aldermen were asked to say what issues they considered most important during a given time period and, later in the conversation, they were asked to name the issues which they thought the public considered most important. In both cases respondents were asked to rank order the issues. To produce the importance rating a point system was used: if an issue was ranked as first in importance, it was assigned a point value of 5; if ranked second, the point value was 3; if ranked third, the point value was 1. The results are shown in Table 3.

The strength of the relationship between the relative orders of importance for aldermen's perception of issues and aldermen's notions of the public's perception of issues was tested using Spearman's Rank Correlation Coefficient test. The test yielded a value of $\rho=0.25$ in the case of Port Arthur and $\rho=0.66$ in the case of Fort William. In both cases these values suggest some relationship of a positive nature, but when the significance of the values of ρ was tested it was found that while the Fort William value was significant at less than the 5 per cent level, the Port Arthur value was not significant enough to conclude that the relationship could not have occurred by chance. Further, the magnitude of the ρ value for Fort William, demonstrates that the relationship there was substantial.

These figures suggest a close relationship between Fort William aldermen's perceptions of the importance of issues and their notions of the public's perceptions of issues, and raise the possibility that the relationship between the two sets of data may be a causal one. The other data from the interviews, however, demonstrated considerable hostility in both councils to the idea of direct, formal communication between aldermen and the public. How, then, in institutional terms, can the difference between the councils be explained? In other words, are there present, in one council, structural or institutional factors which might cause its members to be influenced in their perceptions of the importance of issues by their notions of the views of the public, but which are absent from the other council?

Table 3. Perceptions of Issues, 1968

Issue	Importance Rating by Respondents	Rank	Respondents Perception of Importance Rating by Public	Rank
Port Arthur				
Amalgamation	44	1	16	3
Urban Renewal	24	2	21	1
Mill Rate	8	3	13	4
Ambulance Service	4	4	—	—
District Health Unit	3	5	—	—
Shuniah Plaza/Night Shopping	1	6	5	5
University Expansion	1	6	—	—
Industrial Park	1	6	—	—
Recreation Facilities	—*	—	17	2
Public Works	—	—	1	6
Fluoridation	—	—	5	5
Fort William				
Amalgamation	26	1	16	2
Sewage	9	2	18	1
Water Agreement	8	3	9	3
Health	6	4	—	—
Taxation	5	5	6	4
Paving	4	6	3	5
Form of Gov't	3	7	—	—
Redevelopment	1	8	—	—
FWCI Renovation	—	—	3	5

* Blank: no mention in category

This problem of analysis may be phrased in even more stark terms: there are data to suggest that in one case aldermen feel free to ignore their own perceptions of what the public considers important and that in the other councillors feel constrained by these perceptions. Since it cannot be argued that a positive relationship such as that found among Fort William aldermen necessarily implies a causal relationship, any conclusions here will be both tentative and speculative. But they do suggest fruitful areas for further empirical research.

One should examine, for example, the idea that aldermen are

constrained by the expectation that any great divergence between their views on issues and the views which they attribute to the electorate will adversely affect their chances of re-election. That aldermen may be aware of the existence of such a constraint is suggested by the frequent references to the power of the electorate as an argument against the appropriateness of plebiscites and referenda. But if it is argued that this possibility was not equally strong for both councils, existing as they did in a single, small, homogenous urban area, it is necessary to demonstrate that the flow of information from councillors to electorate was freer in one city than in the other. In other words before the divergence suggested above could affect the voting behaviour of the electorate, the electorate would have to know of its existence. The problem here is one of the effectiveness of public scrutiny of the elected councils and it must be discovered if there were any structural factors which would have made the possible divergence less visible to the electorate in Port Arthur than in Fort William.

The most obvious structural difference between the two councils was in the nature of the committee systems. The City of Fort William employed a city administrator and operated its council by a system of committees-of-the-whole. Port Arthur, on the other hand, operated the more general mayor-council system, with small sub-committees, the chairmen of which were chosen by the Mayor. Under the provisions of the Municipal Act, city council meetings must be open to the public but committee meetings need not be, the decision being at the discretion of the Council. In Fort William, committee meetings were open but in Port Arthur they were closed. It is likely that this difference had an important bearing on the question of visibility and the effectiveness of public scrutiny of the actions of the councils. In the course of the interviews, respondents were asked how they felt about the workings of the committee system of their councils, and the results are shown in Table 4.

Table 4. Attitudes to Workings of Committee Systems

	Port Arthur	Fort William
Satisfied	90%	43%
Dissatisfied	10%	43%
Don't Know	—	14%

When aldermen were asked to elaborate on their attitudes to their committee systems those from Port Arthur expressed, almost unanimously, the view that closed meetings gave them the opportunity to discuss civic business privately without having to consider that the opinions expressed would be communicated, through the press, to the people. The closed committee was variously described in the following terms:

> "It is a chance to discuss freely without having your words repeated by the press. . . . "

> "An opportunity to discuss without being *misquoted* by the press." (emphasis added)

> " . . . people will say things in committee that they wouldn't say in council. They might . . . change their mind, and this doesn't look good if it's brought . . . into the papers."

> "We decide the pros and cons, and then present it to council *the way we want* and cutting out *all really unnecessary discussion.*" (emphasis added)

The respondent in Port Arthur who said, "We have become unpopular because the public does not get the information that it used to when committee meetings were open," was expressing an attitude towards the public relations of the council which was highly atypical and at variance with the views of the great majority of aldermen who were satisfied with the system and content that it reduced the open council meeting, in the words of one of them, to "a rubber stamp procedure."

The relevance of these perceptions of the closed committee meeting to the notion of visibility introduced above becomes apparent when the relationship between the committees and the council in Port Arthur is examined. In the words of one Port Arthur alderman, the typical council meeting lasted "a half hour" every second week. At these meetings the council adopted reports, ratified decisions and passed by-laws presented to it by the chairmen of the various committees. Relevant documents were circulated in advance to aldermen and discussion of them in council was minimal or absent. Press, radio and television coverage of the actions of the council was restricted to reports of decisions taken and interviews with the chairmen of the committees concerned. The council was reluctant to question committee members publicly, and when one alderman described the relationship by saying, "I can't think of any chairman who has brought in a recommendation to our council that has blown up in his face," he characterized the virtually complete delegation of the civic decision-making process to the closed meetings of sub-committees. This delegation certainly produced in Port Arthur a situation where the decision-making process was completely invisible to the electorate and where, to the public, the council invariably presented an appearance of complete unanimity and harmony.

In such circumstances, of course, it becomes less than credible to see the force of public opinion as expressed at the polls as meaningful restraint on the activities of the individual aldermen. To the public, the alderman has no individuality, being simply one part of a unanimous body which, by the dispatch with which it conducts its business, presents a picture of considerable efficiency and managerial expertise. Thus, the institutional structure and *modus operandi* of the council in Port Arthur provides a possible explanation for the lack of significant correlation between aldermen's perceptions of issues and their views of the public's perception of issues.

In sharp contrast to the opinions expressed in Port Arthur, aldermen in Fort William, in a majority of cases, demonstrated a high level of awareness of the effects of the publicity surrounding the deliberations of the council and of its standing committees-of the-whole. However, attitudes to the committee system (see Table 4) revealed considerable ambivalence towards the workings of open committees, and the respondent who said that due to "a colossal lack of responsibility on the part of the committee chairman . . . committee of the whole is the only way we can work" articulated a view which was apparent in the conversations of several respondents: that public scrutiny of the decision making process was not necessarily a good thing, but that given the personalities and issues involved it was the best method of operation for this particular council. This perceptual ambivalence does not, however, detract from the validity of the hypothesis which is being developed on the basis of the statistics (Table 3) and other data. An awareness among Fort William aldermen that the entire decision making process was public and open may be an explanation of the high level of correlation between their perceptions of the importance of issues and their notions of the public's perceptions of the importance of issues.

It may be possible to examine the foregoing findings with reference to the "rule of anticipated reactions." The thesis of "anticipated reactions" or "unintended (or indirect) influence" was propounded by Carl Friedrich[8] and applied by Dahl, Presthus and Jennings in their community studies of New Haven, Edgewood and Riverview and Atlanta respectively. Simply stated, the thesis is that those who wield power are influenced in their decision making by their own subjective notions of how the citizenry will react to the decisions taken. One of the purposes of this thesis is to suggest that influence is not exercised solely by those who participate directly in community affairs, and in the area of local government, where voter participation is often very low, this can introduce a new dimension to the study of influence and community power structures.

Although it might be argued that even in the absence of free elections, the decision making process will be affected by the rulers' anticipations of the reactions of the ruled, for "anticipated reactions" to be considered an *effective* influence or constraint on decision makers demands the possibility that the ruled will be able to institute sanctions against or exact a penalty from the rulers. In other words, elections must be considered to be essential to the applicability of the "rule of anticipated reactions."[9] However, the operational level of the "rule of anticipated reactions" will be affected by the institutional structure of the system. It may be suggested that there are certain operational conditions for the "rule of anticipated reactions":

1. *Substantive*

a) that the electorate has some criteria on which to judge the rectitude of decisions taken;

b) that the electorate has some criteria on which to judge the rectitude of decisions which will be taken;

[8] C. J. Friedrich, *Constitutional Government and Democracy* (New York, 1937); R. A. Dahl, *Who Governs?* (New Haven, 1961); R. V. Presthus, *Men at the Top* (New York, 1964); M. Kent Jennings, *Community Influentials* (Glencoe, 1964). See also, Roy Gregory "Local Elections and the Rule of Anticipated Reactions," *Political Studies*, XVII (1968), pp. 31-47.

[9] See Dahl, *op. cit.*, p. 101.

2. *Procedural*

c) that the electorate has some criteria on which to judge how decisions were taken;

d) that the electorate has some criteria on which to judge how decisions will be taken.

The bases of these operational conditions are, respectively, as follows:

a) publication of decisions;
b) election on the basis of a legislative program that is, almost invariably, a partisan, competitive election;
c) openness of the decision-making process;
d) similar to (b), with candidates (or parties) making an issue of the nature of the decision-making process.

Table 5 shows the operational level of the "rule of anticipated reactions" within various institutional structures.

Table 5. Institutional Structure and "Anticipated Reactions"

Institutional Type	Institutional* Structure	Whether Conditions Operative				Operational Level
		a	b	c	d	
1	Partisan/Open	Yes	Yes	Yes	Yes	Fully
2	Non-partisan/Open	Yes	No	Yes	No	Semi
3	Partisan/Closed	Yes	Yes	No	Yes	Highly
4	Non-partisan/Closed	Yes	No	No	No	Minimally

* "Partisan" is used to indicate that elective offices are regularly competed for on a party political basis; "open" is used to indicate that all formal stages of the decision-making process take place publicly.

If this configuration is applied to the two councils being examined here, it is found that whereas the Fort William council, since elections to it were non-partisan and since both committee and full council meetings were open, was of Type 2, that of Port Arthur, where elections were also non-partisan but where the vital stage of the decision-making process – committee meetings – was closed, was of Type 4 and thus it may be argued that the "rule of anticipated reactions" was semi-operational in Fort William, but only minimally operational in Port Arthur. Thus, there is a further possible explanation for the differences found between the councils in the correlation test of the values given in Table 3.

As well as providing data concerning the perceptions of council members regarding their own role, their relationship with the electorate and the relative importance of issues, the interviews also yielded information on the patterns of influence within the councils and on the sorts and sources of pressure to which aldermen were subject while engaged in the decision-making process. It was indicated above that aldermen were virtually unanimous in their opposition to the entry of party politics into municipal government, but it was also suggested that a number of the interviewees did express a preference for a particular political party. Usually, where a preference was expressed, it had been indulged to the point of party membership and in some cases to the extent of becoming or seeking to become a party candidate for election to the federal or provincial legislature. The incidence of various types of party identification and preference for particular parties in Port Arthur is given in Table 6.

Table 6. Levels of Party Identification – Port Arthur

	Liberal	Prog. Cons.	N.D.P.	None
Identification	—	—	—	5
Membership	1	—	1	—
Sought Candidacy	—	2	—	—
Candidacy	1	—	—	—
TOTALS	2	2	1	5

It will be seen from these figures that the incidence of partisan identification in the Port Arthur council was not high, with half of the members having no firm identification with any party. It is also significant, in view of the aldermen's perceptions of the types of influences which contributed to the decision-making process in the council, that even among those who did identify with a particular party, there was no concentration of support for any one group. In answer to a question about the incidence of party politics as an influential factor affecting council decisions 70 per cent of the respondents replied that it was never a factor and the others said that it hardly ever was. Thus there was, at least at the perceptual level, considerable consistency between the attitudes to the entry of political parties to municipal government and the *modus operandi* of the council in its decision making role. In this context also it is significant that in no case was encouragement from a political party given as a reason for first running for election to Council and that in only one case was the desirability of party representation given as a reason for wishing to remain on council.

Given the fact that, in a federal system, the municipal is the tertiary level of government, it was decided to investigate how far aldermen felt constrained in their decision-making role by policies already established by the higher levels of governments, particularly the provincial. In Ontario, not only are all activities of local authorities governed by the provisions of the Municipal Act, but all major capital expenditures must have the approval of the Ontario Municipal Board, a regulatory body established by the provincial government. Under these circumstances, the degree of variation recorded among the aldermen's responses to the question: "Are decisions taken with reference to the policies of the federal and provincial authorities?" was surprising. Only three Port Arthur aldermen indicated that they felt that the Council was constrained in its decision-making by policies established by the other levels of government, and it is perhaps significant that these three were among the four most influential members of the Council in the perceptions of their colleagues.

Respondents were asked to say which individuals and groups, both inside and outside the Council, they thought had been involved with the most important issues which had come before the Council in the preceding year (see Table 3). The responses to this question indicated that, in the perceptions of Port Arthur aldermen, the only outside group which was greatly concerned with issues which came before the Council in the period under investigation was the business community. For the purposes of this analysis four organizations – the Lakehead Chamber of Commerce (including the Junior Chamber), the Lakehead Executives Association, the Convention Bureau, and the Downtown Businessmen's Association were grouped together to form one interest group and it was found that this group received thirteen nominations, spread over three of the six most important issues, as having been concerned to influence the council in its decision-making role. It is interesting to note that this group was mentioned as having been interested in those issues which might be argued to have a direct bearing on the well-being of the business community, namely amalgamation, downtown urban renewal and the attitude of the council to the new shopping plaza outside the city limits and the night shopping by-law. The outside group which was ranked second in nominations was the Labour Unions; but this group received only three mentions, all of which were on the issue of amalgamation.

The continued influence of the business community in the affairs of the city council became even more significant in view of some of the other data collected. First of all, five members of the council, as well as the mayor, were businessmen and only one of these, an insurance broker, did not operate his own business in the downtown area. Secondly, five members of council, as well as the mayor, indicated that they had been encouraged to run for election in the first instance by business organizations. Thirdly, out of thirty-five nominations in answer to the question, "Which members of the Council do you consider to have most influence on its decisions?" twenty-two went to the five businessmen on the council, and there was a general indication among all respondents that the mayor, also a businessman, exercised an influence on the council's decision-making which was ill-defined but constant.

Among Fort William aldermen there was a much higher incidence of party identification than was found in Port Arthur.

As Table 7 shows, there was, among those interviewed, a heavier concentration of identification with the Progressive Conservative

Table 7. Levels of Party Identification – Fort William

	Liberal	Prog. Cons.	N.D.P.	None
Identification	—	—	—	—
Membership	1	5	—	—
Sought Candidacy	—	—	—	—
Candidacy	1	—	—	—
TOTALS	2	5	—	—

Party, a concentration which would diminish only slightly if the political preferences of those aldermen who were not interviewed were included. Also in contrast to Port Arthur, perceptions of the incidence of party politics as an influential factor in the deliberations of council were varied, with only three of the respondents saying that partisan considerations never entered and two of the others saying that such influence was almost continual, one that it was quite frequent and the other that it was occasional.

In the perceptions of many respondents, moreover, the Fort William council in its decision-making process was characterized by what one alderman called "a government and an opposition" and the incidence of open conflict both in council and in committees-of-the-whole was thought by most respondents to be high. Unlike Port Arthur, where respondents generally (but not invariably) mentioned influential *individuals*, most respondents in Fort William answered the question, "Which members of Council do you consider to have most influence on its decisions?" in terms of *groups* or *alliances* which they considered to be permanent or semi-permanent in nature.

It was thought by some respondents that the contentiousness of council meetings and the formation of alliances among aldermen were causally related to the openness of a decision-making process which allowed press and public to see exactly how particular aldermen acted upon specific issues. Such openness may also help to explain why, again in striking contrast with Port Arthur, there was no perception of any continuing effort by any interest group to influence the decisions taken by council. Such pressure as was exerted during the period under study came from *ad hoc* groups of citizens who presented briefs to the council on such matters as amalgamation, the provision of storm sewers and renovations to one of the local high schools.

Although there was in Fort William no perception among aldermen that there existed a continuing pressure group acting on council in the way that the business community was perceived to act in the neighbouring city, it was found that business organizations received the greatest number of nominations as having been concerned with the important issues during the period under study. The major differences in the two cities were that whereas the business community received thirteen nominations in Port Arthur (an average of

1.3 per respondent), the corresponding group received only five nominations in Fort William (an average of 0.7 per respondent), and that whereas in Port Arthur the nominations were spread over three of the six most important issues, in Fort William the business community was perceived to have been concerned only with the issue of amalgamation.

On the question of the position of the council in its decision making *vis-à-vis* the policies established by the higher levels of government, four of the seven respondents in Fort William thought that the council was constrained by such policies and, in common with the findings for Port Arthur, three of these four were among the four most influential members in the perceptions of their colleagues. These results, therefore, suggest the possibility of the existence of a relationship between influence and knowledge of the procedures and legislative competence of municipal government.

This paper has attempted to present and analyze the perceptions which local aldermen in the councils of two contiguous cities have of their role, of their institutions and of the *modus operandi* of these institutions. It has not attempted to suggest that the findings in Port Arthur and Fort William would be similar to findings in other Canadian cities, but it does indicate that, in the absence of political parties, the distance between the rulers and ruled may be increased and the ability of the electorate to influence the process whereby decisions affecting it are made may be diminished. It also suggests that, in the absence of political parties, the institutional structure of the legislative body may seriously affect the decision-making process and may become an important variable in the analysis of relationship between citizen demands and political actions.

The decision-making process at the municipal level in Canada has not received the academic attention it deserves and it is hoped that this paper may stimulate further study of this aspect of urban politics.

4

Theoretical Implications of Canadian Urban Party Activity

Introduction

Like parties at other levels of government, the urban party provides an important linkage between the citizenry and the political decision-makers. Paradoxically, many Canadian urbanites feel that there is no need for "politics" in local government, rather that local government is purely a matter of administration which does not require political parties as does provincial and federal government. Politics, it seems, is equated with political party activity. Secondly, many persons hold the view that the party system in local government inevitably brings with it graft and corruption. Recently, however, there has been an increasing realization that party systems at the local level serve similar functions that they perform at senior levels of government.

In the first selection, Harold Kaplan develops a typology of electoral and legislative activity in cities with partisan, factional, and non-factional systems. This typology helps us to better understand the relationship between organizational structures and electoral activity.

In the following piece, Peter Silcox argues persuasively that if local government is to be accountable to the electorate, political parties are a necessity. He suggests that a viable, enduring party system at the local level is only possible if local political parties maintain close ties with provincial parties. He maintains that the purely local party cannot survive for any period of time.

In the paper by Stephen Clarkson, the attempt to introduce party politics into previously nonpartisan Metro Toronto elections is likened to the marketing of a new product. He uses economic theory as a framework for analysing the effects of this new "product" in the political marketplace. Clarkson speculates that once organized parties have captured a position on council, they will provide information to voters which will result in parties obtaining an increasing portion of the elective offices.

The selections by Harold Kaplan and James Lightbody provide a fitting conclusion to this final section. Kaplan views the weak leadership in Canada's large cities as a result of the absence of centralized authority in civic affairs. He indicates that party activity would remedy this weakness and at the same time introduce a greater element of responsibility into civic politics. He cautions, however, that the introduction of urban party politics would not be without its dangers including the possibility that cities would become dominated by one party. Lightbody makes a strong case for partisan politics, arguing that the nonpartisan tradition in local government is an anachronism in the increasingly urban Canadian society. He argues that parties in civic politics would produce more responsive government and would provide the necessary innovation and coordination needed to cope with the problems of rapid urban growth.

Electoral Politics in the Metro Area

HAROLD KAPLAN

Classifying Urban Electoral Politics

The most useful way to classify local elections in North America is to place these elections along a structured-unstructured continuum.[1] Where parties or *ad hoc* electoral alliances prepare slates or tickets to guide the voter in his selection, that election may be classified as relatively structured. Unstructured elections exist where no bracketing or grouping of candidates occurs, where party or factional labels are missing, and where each candidate runs his own separate campaign.

Table 1 tries to make this distinction more precise by dividing the electoral process into component activities. . . . Three ideal types of electoral politics – partisan, factional, and non-factional – are constructed and compared to the Toronto area pattern. Each type of election is described in terms of whether the component activities are performed at all and, if so, by whom they are performed.

The most highly structured form of electoral politics exists in partisan cities, even though there are almost endless varieties within this category. The common feature of all partisan elections is that stable, enduring organizations try to win control of city government and to maintain some degree of party unity in the policy-making

From *Urban Political Systems: A Functional Analysis of Metro Toronto* (New York: Columbia University Press, 1967), pp. 181-188. Reprinted by permission.

[1] The structured-unstructured distinction is developed in Oliver Williams and Charles Adrian, *Four Cities* (Philadelphia, University of Pennsylvania Press, 1963), particularly Ch. 3. My references to particular American cities are based largely on descriptions contained in Edward Banfield and James Wilson, *City Politics* (Cambridge, Harvard and M.I.T. Press, 1963).

Table 1. The Performance of Electoral Activities in the Metro Area and in Three "Ideal" Cities

	Actors Performing the Activities			
Electoral Activities	Partisan City	Factional City	Non-factional City	Metro Area
Initiating candidacies	Parties, interest groups and individual candidate	Individual candidate, sometimes factions and interest groups	Individual candidate; sometimes interest groups	Individual candidate
Endorsing candidates	Parties; sometimes interest groups	Factions; sometimes interest groups	Interest groups	Interest groups
Campaign activities: canvassing, getting out vote, etc.	Parties	Factions or individual candidate	Individual candidate	Individual candidate and parties (not all activities performed)
Raising campaign funds	Parties and individual candidate	Factions and individual candidate; sometimes interest groups	Individual candidate; sometimes interest groups	Individual candidate
Preparing slate of candidates	Parties	Factions	Not performed	Not performed
Preparing policy program for slate	Parties (not always performed)	Factions (rarely performed)	Not performed	Not performed
Disciplining legislative voting	Parties (not always performed)	Not performed	Not performed	Not performed

process. The city may be overtly partisan, like New York, or may be ostensibly nonpartisan yet actually dominated by one party, like Chicago. The parties may correspond to the national, state, or provincial parties; on the other hand the parties may operate under labels like "the City Charter Committee" or "the Citizens' Association" and may have no organizational ties to the regular parties in the area.

By and large Canadian political parties do not overtly contest local elections.[2] No Canadian city government is controlled by one of the provincial and federal parties. Only Montreal approaches the degree of structured politics evident in U.S. partisan cities. In Montreal a purely local organization, called the Civic Party, controls a large majority of the seats in city council and maintains voting discipline in council proceedings.

A "faction" will be defined as an electoral alliance that dissolves once the election is over. Factional cities have slates of candidates in local elections but do not have disciplined, party voting in the council. The purpose of the faction is to elect certain individuals to office, not to carry out any policy program or to influence the behaviour of the elected officials on policy matters. This type of election may produce a majority bloc in the legislature but it does not produce a cohesive bloc, capable of governing. The elections are structured, through the use of labels and the grouping of candidates' names on the ballot, but the politics of the municipal council in the period between elections is not structured. Often these factions will dissolve and reappear under different names from one election to another. The voter is presented with a list of factions, but the names may be substantially different than the names of the factions contesting the last city election.

Faction elections occur in several large Canadian cities. The Civic Election Committee in Winnipeg and the Non-partisan League in Vancouver are excellent illustrations of stable but loosely organized alliances, seeking to elect certain types of candidates (non-Socialist, non-Labor candidates) but not seeking to become governing parties. In Edmonton, on the other hand, the names of the factions change from one election to the next.

[2] My remarks about Canadian city politics are based mainly on accounts presented in the Vancouver *Sun*, the Vancouver *Province*, the Montreal *Star*, *Le Devoir* (Montreal), the Winnipeg *Tribune*, and the Winnipeg *Free Press*.

The least structured variety of electoral politics exists in those cities that have neither parties nor factions. Each candidate runs his own campaign, refuses to attach any labels to his name, and refuses to link his name with any other candidates running for different offices. The voter is presented with a ballot consisting of a long list of individual names, in no way formally classified or identified. Non-factional politics prevails in many American cities, like Minneapolis, Detroit, and Los Angeles, and in Canadian cities, like Calgary, Hamilton, Ottawa, and Windsor. Canada apparently contains a larger percentage of non-factional cities than does the United States.

Metro's Unstructured Electoral Politics

Electoral politics in Metro's thirteen municipalities was highly unstructured. Each candidate for local office ran and financed his own campaign, recruited his own organization and campaign workers, ran on his own record, refused to use any labels in the space provided on the ballot, denied affiliation with any of the established parties, and refused to comment on any contests for local office other than his own. Candidates for mayor or reeve studiously avoided involvement in aldermanic contests, and candidates for council seats remained neutral on mayoral contests. There was no mayor's ticket as is the case in some American factional cities.

Factional lines appeared in York Township after a judicial inquiry found irregularities in the town's land dealings. A "reform" faction and an "old guard" faction contested the 1958 and 1960 elections. By 1962, however, York had returned to its traditional non-factional pattern.

Metro area elections also were characterized by an emphasis on personalities rather than issues; an emphasis on detailed, neighbourhood grievances rather than city-wide or town-wide issues; low keyed, sedate campaigns; and a great likelihood that incumbents seeking re-election would be returned. Such features seem more likely to occur in unstructured than structured elections, but Metro area elections were even more issueless and placid than elections in most non-factional cities. It can be seen in Table 1, for example, that some campaign activities performed in my typical factionless cities arose from the failure of Metro groups to provide some structuring of the electoral process.

Rivals for municipal office in the Metro area usually agreed that there were no issues in the contest other than the personalities, honesty, and administrative abilities of the candidates and the question of which candidate has deeper roots in the community. All candidates for a suburban office would denounce total amalgamation, promise to hold the line on taxes and to service neighbourhood requests, criticize inadequate police and transit service, and advocate the attraction of more non-residential assessment to the municipality. Candidates in the city would agree on the shortcomings of the Metro federal system and on the need for more parks, subways, public housing, and downtown redevelopment. Higher levels of government were usually blamed for Toronto's "runaway" tax rate. The major issue in aldermanic contests, in both the city and suburbs, was which candidate had done more or could do more for the neighbourhood. In those suburbs where one person had served as reeve for ten or fifteen years, the challenger would try to make bossism the issue. In larger suburbs an important issue was whether the reeve would come from the northern or southern part of the town.

The most obvious characteristic of voting in Toronto area elections was the tendency to vote for friends and neighbours.[3] A candidate usually polled his strongest vote in the areas where he had been born and raised, where his wife had been born and raised, where he presently lived, and where his office or business was located. Even candidates for a city-wide or town-wide office had their neighbourhood strongholds. This voting pattern suggests that, in the absence of issues or factions, the extent of a candidate's personal, business, and neighbourhood affiliations were crucial factors in electoral success. The candidate with deep social roots in the community, the long-time resident of a neighbourhood with an extensive network of personal relations, was difficult to beat.

Incumbents were also difficult to beat. Voters in Metro apparently responded to the most familiar names, and incumbents usually were better known than challengers. One measurement of the ease with which incumbent officials are returned to office is the incumbency ratio. Of the 180 incumbent Metro councillors who sought

[3]"Friends and neighbours" is a pattern of voting analyzed by V. O. Key Jr., in *Southern Politics in State and Nation* (New York, Alfred A. Knopf, 1949), see particularly Ch. 14.

re-election to municipal office between 1953 and 1965, only 26 were not returned to Metro Council. Thus, the incumbency ratio in the Metro area was approximately .86 – that is, about 86 per cent of the incumbent Metro councillors seeking re-election were returned to the Council. Of the 26 defeated councillors, 13 were Toronto aldermen who dropped to second place in the ward vote and thus lost their Metro seat but not their municipal seat. If these 13 aldermen are treated as incumbents returned to office, Metro's incumbency ratio rises to .93.[4]

Another indication of the security of incumbent officials was the large number of uncontested elections in the suburban municipalities. In a typical election year three or four of the twelve suburban reeves and mayors were returned to office by acclamation. Reeve Dorothy Hague of Swansea was returned to office without a contest in nine consecutive elections. During Forest Hill's first forty-four years as a municipality, less than one-quarter of its elections for reeve were contested. Suburban contests were more likely to occur when an incumbent retired. In addition, offices were contested a bit more vigorously in the larger suburbs.

The Toronto area's campaigns were also more nonchalant than campaigns appear to be in most large American cities. Even in the City of Toronto, where political competition was keener than in the suburbs, campaigning was largely confined to a three-week period. A candidate making his first campaign for electoral office, or an alderman making his first campaign for controller or mayor, might have to spend generous amounts of money to make his name known; but incumbents seeking re-election were able to obtain re-election with minimal campaign expenditures. Candidates, particularly incumbents, often dispensed with certain campaign activities, like door-to-door canvassing, mailing campaign literature, and getting out the vote on election day. This lack of excitement and

[4]The incumbency ratio is used in Charles Gilbert and Christopher Clague, "Electoral Systems in Large Cities," *Journal of Politics*, XXIV (May, 1962), pp. 323-49; and Eugene Lee, *The Politics of Nonpartisanship* (Berkeley and Los Angeles, University of California Press, 1960), pp. 65-66. No exact comparisons between Metro and these studies can be made, since both studies dealt with city councillors. Nor do these studies produce any firm conclusion on the relation between unstructured politics and the security of incumbents. Lee found more security in partisan state elections than in non-partisan city elections. Gilbert and Clague found security to be high in non-partisan cities but highest in one-party cities.

intensity was probably transmitted to the voters. Voter turnout was as low as 20 per cent in some municipalities and rarely exceeded 35 per cent in any municipality.

Group Involvement in Metro Elections

One reason Metro's electoral politics remained more sedate and issueless than electoral politics in other non-factional cities was the failure of interest groups to become involved in Metro elections. In American factionless cities where private groups make endorsements of candidates for local office, the electoral process becomes more structured or meaningful. Issues are thrust into the foreground, and the importance of personalities and personal acquaintances recedes. In these cities the groups step in and fill the vacuum left by the absence of factions or parties. In some cases interest groups defend the exclusion of parties from local elections precisely because these groups are better able to dominate non-partisan elections.[5]

In Metro some groups sought influence over policy making but not over elections. Included in this category were the BMR*, the Board of Trade, the Social Planning Council, AWE†, and most neighbourhood groups. Other groups, mainly the political parties, sought influence in the electoral arena but not in the policy-making arena. There was, therefore, a gap between the policy-making sphere and the electoral sphere. Most Metro interest groups did not try to maximize their influence over elections as a means of enhancing their control over policy decisions. Even the Toronto newspapers and the Labour Council, which *did* make endorsements of local candidates, did not consistently use these endorsements to promote particular viewpoints on policy. This gap between the electoral and policy-making spheres helps explain why Metro groups generally did not try to pressure Metro councillors, why groups in Metro relied more on the persuasiveness of their case than on threats of reprisals at the polls.

[5]For conflict between parties and non-partisan reformers see A. T. Brown, *The Politics of Reform* (Kansas City, Community Studies, 1958); Robert Salisbury, "St. Louis Politics: Relationships among Interests, Parties, and Governmental Structure," *Western Political Quarterly*, XIII (June, 1960), pp. 498-507; S. T. Gabis, "Leadership in a Large Manager City: The Case of Kansas City," *The Annals of the American Academy of Social and Political Science*, CXXXV (May, 1964), pp. 52-63. See also Banfield and Wilson, *City Politics*.

*Bureau of Municipal Research [Ed.] †Association of Women Electors [Ed.]

But the participation of the parties, the Toronto press, and the Labour Council in local elections did give some structure to the electoral process. The description of Toronto area elections as disorganized and personal must be qualified with an account of the electoral roles these groups played. It is also important to know why these groups participated at all and why they did not participate more.

Everybody's Urban Crisis

PETER SILCOX

In Toronto, Robert Macauly is preaching for a call; the "hero" of the 1965 federal election, Senator Davey, is searching for a municipal Trudeau; the N.D.P. is calling out the volunteers yet again; a new local party, C.I.V.A.C., offers "Three Visions of Toronto"; the established councillors have launched an "incumbents" protective association, the C.C.C. In Montreal, Mayor Drapeau leaves his Bingo game to walk through littered streets to announce, "Love me, Love my Exposition." In Vancouver, Premier Bennett is accused of failing to admit that the city exists at all. In Winnipeg, Mayor Juba proclaims the imminent death of the Central City, and abandons the role of executioner to establish a first aid post.

Everywhere Canadians have turned from their TV sets and the interminable programs on the crisis in U.S. cities to discover an urban crisis of their very own. Some Canadians have already been at work on a diagnosis. Provincial governments have investigated structural and financial problems, a few have begun the process of reform. But will this be enough to start Canadians on the road to the solution of functional problems? The chorus of dissent begins to swell. Increasingly the Canadian "Metropolitan Problem" is discussed in terms of the inadequacy of internal decision-making process at the local level. The new reform prescription is dynamic executive leadership; its aim, to awaken public interest, to frame and implement long term plans to reshape the city, and to flush the provincial politicians out of the rural backwoods.

How are we to get a new leadership in Canadian cities which will actually lead? Two methods are being canvassed: the develop-

From *The Canadian Forum*, May, 1969, pp. 36-37. Reprinted by permission.

ment of a strong mayor system, and the introduction of a party system at the local level. I am not sure that these are real alternatives. A strong mayor system would involve a sharp break with Canadian traditions, and drastic action by unwilling provincial governments; the introduction of a party system requires neither. Strong mayor systems require men of exceptional drive and ability; but where are these men to be found? Recent Canadian experience with super politicians has not been a happy one. In any case, the absence of party support for a strong mayor would leave him dependent on powerful special interests. In the Canadian context, that means developers, contractors and the like.

What, then, do parties have to offer? Parties are permanent organizations with permanent bodies of workers. Made up of a cross section of the population, they can act as a two way communication channel to relieve the local councillor from his dependence on the mass media and special interests. In Canadian cities, newspapers and radio stations controlled by big businessmen have gained enormous influence by their near monopoly in this field.

In trying to select good candidates, parties can bring their experience to bear. It is good politics to try to maximize support by promoting candidates from a cross section of the community, and to break the grip of lawyers, small businessmen, housewives and the retired on Canadian local councils. Good men will be attracted by campaign assistance, the promise of purposeful activity and the prospect of promotion within the party.

A party must have a realistic program to offer to the electorate. This should provide a guide to future action, and the basis for the judgement of the party's performance in office. How does one call Juba or Dennison to account when they can point to their relative powerlessness as individuals against a council they will describe as factious and difficult? The citizen must be presented with some clear cut choices: a domed stadium or better street cleaning for the Montrealer, downtown redevelopment or more parks for the citizen of Winnipeg, if he is to participate in local decisions. There is nothing immoral in his limited interest. What a ghastly world it would be if all one's friends devoted their conversation to tracing a path through the complex jungle of local politics.

If Canadian towns are to be decent places to live in the future, they must embrace many changes. Only where there are city-wide organizations asserting the interest of the community as a whole against the special interests of developers and neighbourhood groups alike, can these groups play a constructive role. Parties provide such a disciplined force and protect councillors from intimidation from both developers and groups. A chanting, placard-waving throng of property owners shouting down councillors during council meetings (an increasingly common event in recent years) is a disgrace to any city, not an exercise in grass roots democracy.

Let us look at a number of objections to the introduction of a party system. "The present system works well," says the local mayor. Does it? Are local councils facing the new problems? If they are, why does a large majority of the public feel so dissatisfied? Why are Montrealers in revolt over their rapidly rising tax bills? Why do provincial governments feel bound to intervene so often, and to check municipalities so regularly?

"Sewer construction, road building, snow clearance and other things that local governments control don't involve political issues." What nonsense. What distinguishes these matters from the operation of a welfare system and a national defence system, both of which appear to be fit subjects for politics? Nothing. Any subjects on which large groups of people can disagree are political issues. As long as people can take different sides on an issue, it can be, and is in fact, a political issue. But sewers? Surely the question of whether to replace an existing system of septic tanks, or to spend the same amount of money on another project, say a number of new nursery schools, is a political issue. This is exactly the kind of choice which has to be made every day by local governments. Many of the matters to be decided are, of course, of even greater importance, and involve the great mass of the electorate.

"The present system encourages public spirited citizens to be active in community life. They might not be prepared to join a political party. In any case, parties would bring corruption and private deals into local politics." What evidence is there that political parties are short of high calibre candidates, and that provincial and federal politicians are less public spirited and more corrupt than local politicians?

"The local politician is closer to ordinary people, and more in touch with their needs. In addition, there are no barriers to approaching him." Do you know who your local alderman is? When did you talk to him last, or listen to him explain his position on an issue? If you had a housing problem, would you write to Mayor

Dennison or Paul Hellyer M.P.? Party politicians have just as much interest in keeping in touch with their electorate as independent ones do. The evidence at the federal level is that few people have any inhibitions about asking a party representative for help. In fact, many provincial and federal politicians find they have a vast number of inquiries on local matters, partly as a result of the electorate's lack of knowledge of who the local councillor is, or because of lack of confidence in him.

What kind of party, then: a special municipal one, or the local branches of the provincial one? The first point here is that there probably isn't a real choice. British and American experience with local parties suggests that they simply don't operate successfully for any length of time. When local parties have had limited success, they have been of two types. They may be parties made up of the personal following of a dynamic politician which tends to collapse when he leaves the political arena, and which can be led astray by his pursuit of glory, as is the case in Montreal. Alternatively, they may be hastily-formed coalitions of local interests, formed to deal with a specific problem, or to remove a bunch of crooks. In other cases in the U.S. so-called local political parties are little more than endorsing and campaign organizations, which don't advance a complete program, don't control their members once in office, and don't provide any permanent centre of responsibility or communication. In my view, Canadian local parties are likely to follow this latter model if they are not obliterated soon after their formation. If they do survive, I see little advantage to be gained from their existence.

We can highlight their additional disadvantages by discussing the virtues of provincial parties in local politics. The local branches of provincial parties exist already. They have an organizational structure and a corps of activists. True, where are the mass organizations in Canadian politics? They are conspicuous by their absence. The provincial parties have a pool of politically experienced people, some of whom already sit on councils masquerading as independents, and the experience of selecting suitable people for office. They have knowledge and experience in campaigning, and are recognizable entities to the mass of the public. They are not exclusive organizations; any aspiring politician will be welcomed with open arms. He can get some political training and experience before offering himself for office. They are fund-raising machines, and can afford to promote candidates who are not wealthy enough to finance their own campaigns. This is an important matter. How many Toronto people can afford $5,000-10,000 for an aldermanic campaign, or $30,000 plus for a mayoral one? They have reputations which they are eager to enhance and to protect, so they are very concerned to act responsibly and in a way the public can understand. Finally, they have shown themselves capable of acting in an organized and disciplined manner, when they have won majorities at higher levels.

Canadian parties are not perfect organizations, as any observer of Canadian politics can testify. Winston Churchill once said that democracy was the worst kind of political system, except for all the others. The same might be said of Canadian parties.

Two final objections remain to be considered. One is that people will vote for local parties on the basis of the party's national and provincial images. There is probably some truth in this. British and U.S. experience certainly suggests so. On the other hand, Canadians have shown considerable independence in the past in endorsing different parties at national and provincial levels in a number of provinces. In any case, a party which wins support for its successes at the higher level might seem a good bet at the local level.

Many people have suggested that the situation in which different parties held office at the local and provincial levels would be unhealthy because it would lead to conflict and controversy. Is conflict and controversy unhealthy? Far from it; they are exactly what's needed to stir up interest in the increasingly important subject of municipal affairs and to force well-entrenched provincial governments to pay attention to urban problems. In Ontario, a Conservative government has ruled for 26 years; in British Columbia, Bennett has dominated for 17 years. Would a little more opposition do both a little good? Local governments need not be afraid of the legal superiority of the provinces if they have programs with a popular appeal and develop a real spirit of community involvement. Provincial governments are made up of politicians who need to get elected; they are in no position to act arbitrarily in the face of an aroused public opinion.

If local governments are to solve the problems of rapid urbanization, they need to be shaken up. The purpose of this article is to suggest one method, and I think the best method, of doing just that.

Barriers to Entry of Political Parties into Toronto's Politics

STEPHEN CLARKSON

Defining the Problem

While the rise and fall of political parties has long been a central concern of comparative politics, the birth of parties has normally been seen as the development of new political organizations within parliamentary institutions where parties already exist. The theoretical questions that scholars have asked have accordingly been concerned with such micro-political factors as the influence of the electoral system (whether a single-member, single-vote system discriminates against the entry of the Parti québécois in Quebec's National Assembly), the dynamics of evolving parties (the emergence of the socialist parties by factional splits from the Indian National Congress), or the motivations impelling extra parliamentary movements to transform their activity within the political system (the origins of the British Labour Party).

The entry of parties into non-party political systems has been left to the students either of Western parliamentary development or of the decolonization process in the third world. The treatment of these problems tends to be descriptive and historical. The entry of new political parties into non-party municipal systems such as Metropolitan Toronto raises a number of interesting problems both old and new for political scientists. The creation of municipal wings by two of the three Canadian national parties (the Liberals and the N.D.P., with the Conserv-

From *Canadian Journal of Political Science*, Vol. 4, (June, 1971), pp. 206-223. Reprinted by permission.

Editor's Note: In this essay the author uses economic theory in an analysis of a local political campaign. It should be noted that the author was a Liberal candidate for mayor in the 1969 Toronto election.

atives waiting on the sidelines) provides new information on the internal evolution of the national parties in response to the emerging consciousness of our "urban crisis." The creation of these new parties plus the simultaneous development in Toronto of a party that is formally not related to the national parties, the Civic Action party (Civac), provides an interesting opportunity for studying the problems of party politics in a municipal system on a comparative basis. As a problem in municipal government, the entry of parties into Toronto's politics raises questions concerning the stage of political development of municipal political systems: is it the size, the complexity, the growing political stakes, the public awakening to a city crisis, or a shift in behaviour towards a greater citizen participation that has created the pressure for party activity?

Equally fascinating about the Toronto phenomenon are the difficulties encountered by the parties trying to penetrate a political system that has until now operated without parties.[1] What one would have expected to be the very easy transposition of political activity from the federal and provincial levels to the municipal arena in the same region within the same nation-state, turned out to be a case of systematic conflict in which the parties encountered real opposition even from within their own ranks. In the heat of political battle they found the municipal arena to be a separate political culture in many ways hostile to their own style, attitudes, and patterns of behaviour. Although geographically almost co-terminous, the municipal political systems are distinct from the provincial and federal in many important ways. The attempted entry of these three parties into Toronto politics thus raises the macro-political problem of parties from one parliamentary system trying to enter the political structures of another, non-party system.

The political science literature dealing with this problem is meagre. The static framework of structural functionalism sheds no light on the dynamic problems of this systemic change. Theories of modernization will not put our finger on what are the critical factors in the "modern" city's "traditional" resistance to political innova-

[1] Municipal politicians have long had personal ties with the national parties, but have till now felt it expedient to conceal these relations in order to appeal to as broad a cross section as possible of the few voters who take part in municipal elections.

tion. It is the economists, in developing a theoretical structure for analysing the penetration of markets by outside firms, who have been more concerned with this type of structural change. Their major categories, identifying the "barriers to entry" that market structures set up to oppose the entry of outside firms, put the problems concerning party penetration into a useful analytical perspective. According to the theory of the firm as it is generally presented in the economic literature, we can identify seven key propositions:

1. The potential entrant's inducements to entry will vary depending on the state of the market and the objectives of the invading firm.

2. The degree of competition in the market will determine the tactics of a potential entrant and the market response to his entry attempt.

3. The specific characteristics of the local market are also of direct importance in affecting the outside firm's ability to adapt his product to local needs.

4. Differentiating his product from those of the existing producers by his mastery of advertising and public relations will be a crucial factor to success.

5. The concept of "consumer sovereignty" implies that the consumer will pass a rational judgment and decide the fate of the new entrant.

6. The strength of the potential entrant – financial, technological, and organizational – will account for his ability to survive.

7. The quality of his product is both alpha and omega of new entry and growth.

Without for a moment accepting the crude equation of election campaigns with selling soap, this conceptual model does give us a framework for analysing the critical problems involved in the penetration of the non-party city political system by political parties. By examining each of these micro-economic propositions in turn, we can see how each applies to the phenomenon of party penetration. We will briefly summarize the generally accepted theory of the firm and then analyze the 1969 Toronto election experience in its terms.

1. Inducements to Entry

According to the theory of the firm, potential entrants are induced into a market because the stakes are high. Prices may be high, allowing super profits and attracting new competitors. A firm may have a new product with which it thinks it can penetrate a new market. A group may even split off from an existing market. The reasons and objectives for new entry are important, for they will determine the strategy of entry.

In Metro Toronto's election campaign of 1969 four parties were officially engaged in seeking seats on municipal councils and boards of education. The League for Socialist Action was a Trotskyite party of mainly young dissidents from the N.D.P. who ran a brave campaign complete with a mayoralty candidate. Of the three "serious" parties, Civac was a coalition drawn from both the national parties and non-party sources, while the Liberals and N.D.P. had established municipal wings to contest the election with autonomous electoral organizations and separate ward associations. In terms of their motivation to enter city politics they were, practically speaking, identical as three expressions of a general reform movement in the city. As their platforms indicate, they shared a common ideology. They opposed the existing system of institutionalized individualism in which the elected representatives were not genuinely accountable to the public for lack of structures controlling their performance after election. The institution of party was presented as a means of imposing discipline and accountability on the elected representatives through a democratically run, city-wide political structure open to participation by any interested citizen or group. Philosophically, they agreed on a broadly populist conception of the city: the city is for people; "quality of life" problems should take precedence over "quantity of concrete" solutions; expressways, new apartment construction, and urban renewal need bringing under control as they threaten the quality of the urban environment. The concept of community dominated their approach to policy-making: schools should be responsive to the needs of the local community; planning should be controlled by the neighbourhoods affected. A technocratic note entered the discussion of transportation, which should be planned on an integrated, not a fragmented basis. Finally a touch of city-state feeling was present: City Hall must have more constitutional and fiscal power; elected representatives of better quality should have more responsibility to develop their own solutions to Toronto's specific problems.

While the primary inducement to entry was the felt need for city reform in a period of urban crisis and weak, ineffective city government, there were secondary motivations for the national parties. For the N.D.P. and, to a lesser extent, for the Liberals, municipal party activity would be a means to strengthen organization, increase recruitment, and identify with local problems for the purpose of subsequent provincial and federal election campaigns. However, both parties were hampered by serious internal opposition to municipal activity. The N.D.P. had the longest roots in city politics, having run candidates in 1966, but the Toronto Labour Council's strong support for the incumbent mayor William Dennison, a stubborn opponent of party politics, prevented the N.D.P. from nominating a party candidate for mayor and so running a full campaign with a clearly identified captain.

The Liberals' decision to enter municipal politics was made less than a year before the campaign began and without complete party consensus, with the result that organization, finance, and candidate selection were improvized under the pressure both of the clock and of internal party tensions. For Civac, party organization and ideology were expressly divorced from federal or provincial links, although many individuals had a clear party identification in provincial or federal politics. As the party had been generated at the municipal level it had the initial advantage of more identification with city politicians, but the subsequent disadvantage of suffering numerous withdrawals by incumbents as they assessed the electoral costs of a party label.

The inducement to entry was thus the "profit" to be gained in the form of political reform. The strategy chosen was gaining power through the ballot box, not just with better people, but with politicians working as disciplined groups able to implement a whole program because they had been elected as a team with a mandate to implement their platform. The major barriers to party penetration were found primarily in the radically different "market" with which the municipal electoral system confronted the fledgling parties.

2. Degree of Competition

The difficulties of new entry vary with the type of market, a monopoly being the most difficult to penetrate, a perfectly competitive market being the easiest. The monopolist with total control over pricing and marketing will also be able to influence other factors such as advertising and distribution mechanisms in his counter-attack against prospective competition. In a free market the relative power of the individual producer is too insignificant to affect market conditions and so respond to new challenges in an organized way. In oligopolies where a small number of firms divide up the market, coalitions can be formed to resist unwanted intrusion by price fixing or trade restraints, though a sufficiently powerful new entrant may be able to force himself into the club.

At first glance the city political system appears to be a free market. Since there are no overt parties, each alderman or trustee is elected by virtue of his own local campaign, his personal image, and his individual record. Once elected the individuals vote on issues "according to their consciences" in constantly changing groupings. If this picture corresponded to reality, then new entry by individuals should be easy and new entry of organized groups of individuals should be easier still. It is true that some of the system's characteristics substantiate this free market image. Any citizen on the tax rolls, for instance, can run for public office by following a simple nomination procedure without even having to pay a deposit.

On closer inspection, however, the system reveals many features of the monopoly. As the popular expression "old guard" denotes, city politicians as a collectivity are seen to be a block. They act as individuals, of course, but work as a group in a sheltered market with their seats protected by other characteristics of the system that discourage political competition. City Hall officials necessarily develop close working relationships with the incumbents who thus establish an exclusive access to expertise concerning municipal problems – information that is not so readily available to non-elected political activists, to say nothing of the general public. Businesses with interests in City Hall activities – primarily construction and high-rise housing development – form working relationships with the elected representatives either directly in piloting their particular projects through the City Hall bureaucracy or indirectly with their legal, insurance, or real estate operations outside the formal jurisdictions of City Hall. Incumbents naturally receive the most favourable response from such vested interests when asking for contributions to electoral campaign expenses.

Far from being the hearth of local democracy, open to all interested citizens, City Hall reveals many analogies to restrictive trade practices. Despite an aura of free competition, City Hall was seen at least by the potential entrants as a closed system that had to be taken either by frontal assault or by infiltration. Finding allies from within the system to support the party cause was not easy since incumbents who had not rejected party politics out of hand carefully refrained until the last moment from making a decision for or against their involvement in city parties. This left the parties in the situation of having to launch a frontal attack on City Hall as new entrants. The parties' resultant reliance on outsiders is most clearly illustrated in their policy-making process, which was carried on by groups of reformist younger professionals (town planners, architects, professors, party activists) working in discussion groups throughout the preceding spring and summer to put together the municipal equivalent of a national or provincial party platform. These programs reflected their outsider origins in their generality, their long-range perspective, and their reformist assumptions. This may have been an advantage in differentiating the parties' appeal from the old guard, but did little to make the parties' message better attuned to the political wave-length of city politics.

If the parties' problems were considerable given the monopoly they were tackling, they were noticeably increased by the local characteristics of Toronto's political system.

3. The Nature of the Local Market

Quite apart from the degree of competition in a market, local factors can create decisive barriers to new entry. The tax system may make it impossible for a foreign-controlled company to operate in the local market. The business laws in effect locally may require the potential entrant substantially to alter his way of operating. Local cultural characteristics may require the product to be sold with very different techniques. Geographical or climatic conditions may require major alterations in the firm's product.

While the municipal activists in the national parties were aware of the difficulties involved in cracking city politics, no one probably anticipated their extent. While in theory the parties would bring to campaigning the advantages of their provincial and federal experience, they came up against institutional, legal, and cultural obstacles which made it extremely difficult for them to bring these advantages to bear.

Franchise Restrictions

The parties found the electoral system in Toronto was completely different from that at the provincial and federal levels. One man did not necessarily have one vote. He could have several even if he was not a resident but had several business operations; he might have none if he had not occupied sufficiently elaborate accommodations in the city for a long enough time. Some citizens thus found themselves excluded from the voters' lists in the 1969 campaign while non-citizens appeared on this list. The extreme complexity of the franchise meant that many eligible voters did not think they had the vote – particularly those brought up in smaller towns where only property owners are enfranchised. A second strike against voter activity was the enormous error in the voters' lists. Due to the method of using the tax rolls to establish the electoral lists, their probable average error was 20 per cent.[2] The means of redress were so inadequate that many of those who did know how to request inclusion on the list still were unsuccessful in being registered. While the state of the franchise was publicly deplored by all candidates it was a particular impediment to the parties whose success depended very largely on persuading the whole citizenry to become involved in city politics. The massive initial disenfranchisement of eligible voters and the institutional obstacles to later voter registration hampered efforts to sell the new political product to that two-thirds of the potential consumers who had traditionally kept out of the city political market.

[2]The tax rolls are drawn up between January and September; according to the deputy city clerk, these rolls change by 40 per cent each year. Thus the electoral list drawn up in October is on the average six months out of date or in error by about 20 per cent, or ninety thousand voters. This error was confirmed by Professor Jerry F. Hough in his careful investigation of three wards: "The Liberal Party and the 1969 Toronto Mayoralty Election," paper presented to the Canadian Political Science Association annual meeting, June 4, 1970, mimeo.

The Ballot

Those who exercise a vote in Toronto have an extraordinarily complicated act to perform. Rather than mark a single "x" to record a combined preference for party, policy, leader, and local representative as he does in provincial and federal elections, the municipal voter in Toronto makes at least five separate decisions. He votes for two aldermen to represent his ward in City Council, two trustees to represent his ward on the Board of Education, and one mayor for the city. The implications of this ballot are serious for any party team work. The fortunes of leader and team are separated in the election booth: local candidates campaigning for themselves have no built-in self-interest apart from party loyalty in campaigning for their leader. Preferences for the Liberal mayoralty candidate were not necessarily reflected in support for the Liberal aldermanic candidates and vice-versa. The differentiation of the mayor as a separately elected officer militates against party leaders running for office: it is less risky to run as a local aldermanic candidate who is also leader of a party (the N.D.P. and Civac tactic in 1969) than to run for the all-or-nothing position of mayor and face being left without any office upon defeat (the Liberal tactic). Yet not fielding a mayoralty candidate drastically reduces media coverage for the party effort. At the ward level the strains of running four candidates for election to the Council and the Board of Education are very great. This "team" is composed of two pairs of candidates who are mutually competitive for votes. If there is strong opposition, then the two party candidates may really be vying for one seat on the Council or the Board. Even if both candidates of one party are strong, they will still be competing with each other for the greater political power that comes from topping the ward's poll and getting a seat on Toronto's Metro Council, which has the major powers of government over the six urban boroughs in the whole metropolitan area. It may be more prudent for a party to run only one candidate per ward, but this would make it impossible for the party to obtain a majority on City Council.

Toronto's congressional type of political system led to a particular stress on the individual council record of the incumbent aldermen and mayor. Voting records complied by CORRA, the Confederation of Residents and Ratepayers Associations, underlined the electoral advantage of the incumbent. "Where were you?" was the implicit question asked of new party candidates, for whom caucus solidarity on a platform, not individual performance in council, was the critical factor.

Compared to the single choice ballot of the parliamentary election, the municipal voter has to make a decision on a large number of offices and a huge number of names. The gross inadequacies of communication in giving the voter a good knowledge of the twenty or more candidates in his ward make the difficulty of the electoral choice all the more acute. The result is another obstacle to change: a disincentive to vote. The view was often expressed and reported that there are so many candidates "I cannot distinguish between them and so will not vote."

City Hall's Impotence

The multiplicity of candidates and electoral offices is in inverse proportion to the amount of power that is at stake in municipal election. Even if the voter understands the highly complex division of powers and responsibilities in the political system of Metro Toronto, he is asked to make decisions on relatively minor offices in the overall picture. He is electing aldermen to a council that controls only 20 per cent of his municipal tax dollar, and school trustees who are in a subordinate position to the Metro school board. The mayor he is electing has little more political power than the aldermen, for he is only one of a dozen on the Metro executive committee. The candidates that the voter elects have virtually no control over such central municipal bodies as the transportation commission, police commission, harbour commission, parking authority, and many others. Although the media and the public meetings demand full policy positions of candidates on all issues, these men and women are seeking office for posts that give them only partial influence over the politics for which they may be elected. The aura of irrelevance and impotence that infuses the municipal election atmosphere must be counted as a further psychological obstacle to the entry of parties whose message is that City Hall should be powerful and must have its structure totally transformed.

Multiple Elections

Facing a metropolitan system with six different elections being held simultaneously in Metro's six municipalities, the parties were vulnerable to attack in a way that independent candidates were not. Policy differences between one incumbent and another are not seen to have any more significance than a disagreement between two individual candidates for public office. On the other hand, policy differences between Toronto Liberals and North York Liberals on a matter such as the Spadina Expressway were seen as reducing the credibility of both groups. In trying to run a Metro-wide campaign, a party is liable to be attacked on the platform and in the press for the same disagreements that are accepted as common currency between other candidates.

While the parties suffered from bad press over controversial issues, they were not able to profit from their strength – having a coherent and progressive platform for Metro as a whole. Yet the lack of direct election to Metro Council, the real centre of power, prevented campaign debate on Metro-wide issues. Debate centred instead on the local concerns of ratepayers to the virtual exclusion of Metro problems.

Election Day Procedures

If the parties thought that they would bring in the superior campaigning techniques learned over long years at the provincial and federal levels, they were to be frustrated by the by-laws concerning election day procedures. Since canvassing techniques identifying favourable potential voters depend for their success on monitoring who has voted, regulations forbidding scrutineers to report back to campaign headquarters the names of those who have not yet voted prevented party workers from capitalizing on the whole canvassing effort. Also, the fixing of election day on December 1, a time of year likely to have the worst weather, militates against high voter participation in the election.

If a low voter turnout favours the incumbent, and if the challenging parties required a large response from their federal or provincial supporters as was commonly assumed, then any factor reducing electoral participation *ipso facto* impeded the parties' entry. The rules of the local market created conditions quite foreign to anything the parties had encountered before.

4. Product Differentiation

A firm's success in entering a new market will often depend upon not just the quality of its product but its ability to differentiate this product in the eyes of the consumer. The two factors are not necessarily related: a good new product may not be recognized as such by the consumers and therefore not purchased; a fundamentally similar product, such as a detergent, may be marketed with sufficient originality in label and publicity that it does win a place on the supermarket's shelves.

The entering party's problem in "product differentiation" is communicating to the voter a policy, an image, a style, a personality that genuinely expresses the party's nature and successfully distinguishes its message from rival groups or individuals.

Advertising Resources

The big difference between a party campaign and a firm's strategy is that the latter will not engage a campaign without sufficient funds for advertising. Parties made strategy decisions regardless of financial problems, which were only dealt with once the campaign had been launched. Hence, their first barrier to entry in the field of product differentiation was insufficient money to give them control over sufficient advertising resources to get their message across to the public on television, radio, and in the printed press. It is debatable whether advertising could have transmitted the elaborate policy message that the parties had to communicate, but it is generally agreed that sufficient funds would allow at least a simple political message to be "sold." Not having these funds – and new parties are unlikely to be wealthy if they are reformist – they had to rely on their news-making ability in order to transmit their message to the public.

The parties had a desirable and distinct product in two senses: they had a more elaborate policy platform than individual candidates for any office; they also offered an instrument to implement those policies, namely party discipline in City Hall. If they did not succeed in transmitting this double message to the public it was largely due to the second barrier to product differentiation, the nature of the news media.

Media Relations

To be reported in the three media of communication (television, radio, and press) the parties had to make "news." One characteristic of news is that it must be seen by the reporter to be *new*. Since a position is no longer considered new once it has been reported, it is extremely difficult to sustain media coverage of an issue and adequately transmit the message to a generally uninterested public. The New Democratic Party tried to make the island airport project a major issue, but, once the original spectre had been raised and some mileage made of its dangers in the press, it faded from view since nothing "new" developed. The Liberals made a major attempt to introduce drug abuse as a policy issue both in the Board of Education and in City Hall. Though this was a burning problem at the time in the city, it was not an issue that lasted in the campaign for more than a few days. Not only was it hard to sustain an issue, it was difficult to get a policy position adequately transmitted in the media. A fairly elaborate Liberal policy on the thorny issue of amalgamation was briefly reported following a detailed press conference. There was no way that the public could receive a full explanation of Liberal policy on how a Metro parliament would resolve the basic institutional problems of the city. The party might distribute a brochure to every household but this document could only devote a dozen simple words to the Metro parliament.

A further obstacle to transmitting the parties' policy message was the entertainment imperative of news reporting. Stories had to be linked to personalities preferably in some sensational way. A confrontation between two candidates over a policy issue would be reported as a personality clash, not a debate on the policy questions. Though the parties had entered the city campaign to challenge the political system, the image that was transmitted by the media was simply that of many new candidates, incidentally with party labels, who had come into the fray. The unprecedented phenomenon of candidates working as a team across the city in support of an agreed common program was not conveyed. Whether the message could have been conveyed in a nine-week campaign even had the media decided to give the election higher priority in visual and verbal coverage, is open to debate. This speculation only underlines the point that a significant barrier to entry was the parties' lack of power to ensure that the message they were bringing to the public was communicated in the way they wanted.

The City Hall press gallery itself must be considered alongside the structural and technological qualities of the media as a barrier to entry. The two or three dozen reporters for the three media are themselves part of the system they are assigned to report on. Some have developed their informational source with incumbent politicians and therefore tend to have a stake in preserving the *status quo*. They grow to accept the way the system works and tend to observe the potential entrant in the same light as do the incumbents: a threat to the established way of carrying on city business. This is not to impugn any motives. It is simply to recognize that a further barrier to entry is not being part of the system and so not having the connections and status with the media men that would generate equal space in reporting. Since newsworthiness is defined partly in terms of how well-known is the personality who is making the news, incumbents will almost always get more space than newcomers. If something only becomes newsworthy once it is seen by a reporter, the incumbent again has the advantage by having direct personal access to the media men whose typewriters, microphones, or studios are within a few moments' walk of his own office. Apprehensions that the institution of the party caucus would reduce the amount of information that elected representatives would transmit to the press underlay much of the disparagement with which some reporters treated the party campaigns. Partly counteracting these costs were the benefits of newness: some reporters did welcome the prospect of reform and did try to be fair to the new entrants.

The more identified a reporter was with the system, the more difficult it was for him to see the general and long-term questions that the parties raised in their campaigns. The difficulty the parties experienced in raising fundamental questions such as the redefinition of the role of the cities in the constitution and the general responsibility of the province for city problems may have been due to this factor. A most dramatic example of the differing treatment accorded incumbents and challengers was a CBC series of daily twenty minute interviews of the four mayoralty candidates during the last week of the campaign. The order in which they were presented was in itself deliberate – beginning with the one considered least likely to win (the Socialist candidate) and ending with the incumbent mayor, considered most likely to win and so interviewed last in the series – or closest to the election date. The two party candidates were attacked with extraordinary vigour if not venom by the interviewers, who then proceeded to interview the incumbent controller and mayor with normal politeness and passivity. The general policies of the media towards the campaign were formulated by editors and media executives. The resulting low extent of media coverage further reinforced the psychology of third-class status which plagues the city's politics. Despite the heroic efforts of the news personnel who worked within the budgetary and space limits imposed on them, they could do nothing to rectify the low priority given to the election campaign. The CBC refused to give any free time on television or radio; the newspapers gave little photographic space and refused to open their page seven for policy statements on the grounds that either the news reporters were covering them enough or that they would then have to open their columns to all candidates.

Where media coverage was best, at the mayoralty level, the message was still obscured. One private radio station held an hour long debate among the candidates for mayor; the private television station held a half-hour debate; the *Toronto Star* staged a grilling debate which it printed verbatim. While major efforts were made by the media to be rigorously fair in these events, and they did convey the policy stands of the mayoralty candidates, they did so without being able to transmit the real innovation of party politics being proposed for City Hall. While the mayoralty effort was transmitted in terms of personality, other aspects of the campaign were hardly reported at all. Ward campaigns and borough campaigns received far less coverage, and again in terms of personality rather than party.

Direct Public Meetings

Even such means of direct personal communication with voters as public all-candidate meetings were little more successful. The constraints of time and structure preventing debate between candidates and restricting meetings to brief monologues followed by questions did nothing to help convey the decisive difference party activity would make in City Hall. There was in fact no way convincingly to convey the message that, for the first time in the city's history, candidates were running for all offices – trustees, aldermen, and mayor – behind a common program that they had worked out together in caucus. It was difficult for the voter in Ward 5 to realize that, for the first time, those people who voted N.D.P. in Ward 10 were also voting for the same policies as those voting N.D.P. in Wards 1 through 11. What is a common assumption of parliamentary elections in federal and provincial politics was politically meaningless in the city election.

If full information concerning all products for sale is a defining characteristic of pure competition, the marketplace of Canadian city politics is decidedly impure and resistant to political innovation of so basic a kind as new party politics. A further problem raised by our analogy is that product differentiation will be more difficult if a number of new firms with generally similar policy "products" simultaneously try to enter a market. To some extent it may be argued that the parties, weak as they were, strengthened the cause of party politics by entering the market at the same time. Since, however, the stakes were fixed by the number of seats on Council and the Board of Education, inter-party competition reduced the credibility of any party gaining a majority or even a dominant position. If the supply of voters is inelastic – and the election day returns showed that it had even shrunk from 39 per cent to 35 per cent of the registered voters – then the inter-party competition apparently produced a further disincentive to vote and so weakened the thrust of party entry.

It was hard to determine how successful was the parties' product differentiation in the political marketplace. Was "party" seen to be a package of policies, a team of candidates, a leader or a method of activity in City Hall, or a mix of these attributes? Was the image of entering parties that of inexperience or youthful vigour? Was it of divided parties or of pioneering parties? The way the parties were perceived depended on a host of factors beyond the control of the parties themselves: the federal or provincial party loyalty of the voter, his interest in city politics, the attitude of the newspaper he read, his favourite radio and television stations, or even the attitudes of friends and associates.

With all these uncertainties about the parties' differentiation of their own images, it is not surprising that they were not able to identify specific markets and single out special groups in the public. They had insufficient resources to advertise. They could only carry out "consumer" attitude research within the narrow limits set by telephone polls and canvass questionnaires. The parties could fall back on voter lists from provincial and federal campaigns where the files were in good condition and the constituency executives were sympathetic. Nevertheless, the party faithful refused to turn out: known N.D.P. supporters in Scarborough, for instance, refused to vote on election day despite canvassers' urgings.

5. Consumer Sovereignty

In the final analysis, according to classical economic theory, it is the consumer who is sovereign. The purchaser, by his decision to buy or not to buy a new product, determines the fate of the potential entrant into a new market.

Just as few modern economists will claim that the concept of the sovereign consumer bears much relationship to the real world of the manipulated, indoctrinated, and bribed housewife, there are few political scientists who will defend the simple democratic theory that elections are decided by rationally deliberating men and women. In the present case irrational elements entering into many voters' decisions have been mentioned already. The uncertainty of the franchise, the complexity of the ballot, the impossibly long list of candidates, the lack of knowledge of how the individual candidates stood: these were factors, which together with the cold weather, help explain why the voters stayed away from the polls.

Other factors certainly played their part. The general disinterest in "third rate" City Hall politics because of its apparent irrelevance to their lives was a massive disincentive to participation that could not be counteracted during a brief campaign. So was the general satisfaction with the degree of services provided by City Hall in the traditional areas of garbage collection, sidewalk repair, and snow removal. If City Hall is seen by the vast majority as reasonably efficient and incorrupt, why bother taking an active interest? The scepticism about politics that is latent at the federal and provincial levels came out openly in the municipal campaigns as a general hostility to parties. Despite the reform parties' intentions and claims to the contrary, many people saw them as the instruments of corruption, the means of keeping power from the people, and the agents for politicians to feather their own nests after elections. A different concern expressed was that the election of a particular party to power in City Hall might generate conflict with Queen's Park at the provincial level and produce more costs than benefits.

Even for the fully informed, ideal voter there were genuine causes for doubt. No party had a full-scale effort in every borough across Metro; no party was united on its policy issues when they did cross Metro boundaries. Party candidates were often low in experience and quality. Furthermore the parties seemed to get into more trouble than it was worth: the provincial Liberals issued their most unpopular position paper for extending state support to separate Roman Catholic high schools three weeks before the election in once Orange Toronto.

If the consumer was sovereign in city politics, he was a consumer thoroughly indifferent to the whole system and largely beyond the reach of the press and television set. The sovereign voter was as unimpressed by the N.D.P. campaign literature as by the editorial endorsement of the Liberals in the *Globe and Mail.* With the mayor receiving 45 per cent of a 35 per cent turnout, voter sovereignty meant that the chief officer of Toronto was elected by fifteen per cent of the electorate. The election returns provide a once-for-all consumers' decision that leaves no room for stepping up the advertising campaign or developing new window display. It is a short, sharp, and brutal verdict giving the victors the few spoils of office and leaving the losers out in the cold until the next election campaign warms up.

6. Power of the Firm

Integral to the success of the firm in its new endeavour is the organizational, financial, technological, and commercial strength of the firm itself. A large international firm with massive research departments and adequate means for survey research on the markets will normally be far better able to assault the positions of a tightly defended oligopoly. Financial power and economies of scale will affect the new firm's prospects. A small firm with weak financial reserves and too ambitious a program will quickly fail in its endeavours.

It is in the comparison with the monolithic firm making a well-researched decision to attack a new market that our analogy with party entry is most revealing. For the parties' operations are far removed from the single-minded corporation operating with an efficient command structure in response to policy decisions made carefully in advance.

In theory the national parties should bring many advantages to city politics. For economies of scale, read advantages of concentrating federal and provincial workers on city wards for campaigning. For special skills, patents, and technical expertise, read the advantages of information and experience, that come from close personal ties with the federal and provincial levels for making policies on important city issues. For brand identification, read the impact of the well-known labels "Liberal" and "N.D.P." in the city election. On almost all these points, however, the barriers to entry came not from the civic political system but from the parties themselves. Rather than the centralized firm well prepared to launch a properly financed, carefully orchestrated campaign, the parties were internally split, ill-prepared, improvizing, and uncertain in their first official venture into the city forum.

Finance

Even on so basic a problem as finance, the municipal Liberal party entered the election campaign with no finance committee and $2,000 in debt. The funds promised to the N.D.P. from the Toronto Labour Council did not materialize in the guaranteed dimensions.

Solidarity

Party cohesion was not the expected asset because of the large amount of opposition to party involvement in municipal politics that was still actively expressed inside both the N.D.P. and Liberal parties. Coming primarily from those closely connected with incumbents in municipal politics, dissension within riding and central executives reduced the availability of talent and undermined the confidence necessary for an enthusiastic party campaign.

Local Lore

The expertise with which the party people were meant to approach the election campaign because of their previous federal and political campaign experience was offset by their ignorance of local political lore. Paying for bingos in the name of your candidate at community and ethnic group meetings, for instance, or initiating meetings with the editorial boards of the three newspapers to try to gain their endorsement of each aldermanic candidate was a matter of course for local political figures but out of the realm of experience of the federal or provincial politicians.

Recruitment

In theory, it would be easier to recruit candidates to be part of a team with a central organizational base and financial support. The parties were too embryonic to have established even tolerably acceptable standards for party discipline, qualities for candidates, and methods of campaigning. The open ward associations established by the Liberals' excessively decentralizing constitution were ripe for takeover by any ambitious extrovert interested in a fast way into politics. With little effective role in selecting their aldermanic and trustee candidates, the party leaders had difficulty forming a coherent whole from their very haphazardly selected team mates.

7. The Quality of the Product

The corollary of consumer sovereignty is the notion that no amount of advertising or packaging will save a low quality product. Even if a new product secures a place in a market, it may need to be developed and improved if it is to establish its place in the changing market. The product must be good; it must also answer the needs of the consumers.

The assumptions under which all the parties set up shop and contested the municipal election of 1969 in Toronto were that the city's political system needed rationalization and democratization and that political parties could best meet this need. Other axioms are conceivable. One could agree that there is a need for democratization without positing that parties can provide the answer or the only answer. Those who ran as independents took this line. A more drastic assumption is that the city's problems cannot be resolved unless basic structural changes are made in the whole socio-economic system. The conclusions to be drawn from the campaign and the election are ambiguous. Does the 65 per cent abstention rate justify the latter assumption? Or are the needs for reform simply not yet perceived by the public?

The actual results of the election may appear at first sight to justify the parties' assumption: seven aldermen of the "old guard" were unseated; of the twenty-two aldermen elected to City Council ten were party candidates. Yet these results exaggerated the success of the parties' effort. Of the five alderman who claimed membership in Civac, only three had put any emphasis on their party membership during the campaign. Of the party members elected, most were elected more on the basis of their status as notables in their community. Some claimed they had been damaged by their party label. The underlying reason for the large turnover at City Council was a radical change in ward boundary lines, which left some of the old guard without a ward in which they were genuine incumbents. The most crushing indicator was the low voter turnout, 4 per cent lower than the previous election. The parties had clearly failed to draw into the city political marketplace that silent two-thirds of the electorate who had traditionally voted with their feet – by being unwilling to walk to the polls. Were these factors to be interpreted as judgments on the parties *qua* parties or on new local parties that were fielding very raw candidates? Would the results have been different if there had been an explicitly conservative party contesting the election and providing a real choice from among the parties?

The newness of the parties at the municipal level made the election a first response to the new product. There had been no chance for adaptation of the national parties to local conditions – a process that may now take place in the inter-electoral period.

Conclusion: Crystal-Gazing at the Model

The analysis of the various barriers that confronted parties in their attempt to enter city politics makes it quite clear that it was too much to expect a successful transformation of City Hall in one campaign. Whether the parties will continue to act as agents of change in the local system or be co-opted by the system while they are still in their growing stage will depend both on the kind of party activity that is maintained between elections and on the changing needs of the system itself. If our analytical model is a useful one, it should allow us to make certain statements about the probable course of developments based on each of our seven propositions derived from the theory of the firm.

Inducement to Entry

We should expect parties to continue to concentrate their efforts on municipal politics if the underlying inducement remains – the growing sense of crisis in the cities and the continuing clash between the proponents of growth by concrete construction and the advocates of an improved quality of life. The growing dimensions of such potent issues as the Spadina Expressway controversy promise well to keep the feeling of crisis close to the surface. The resulting political activation of citizen groups between elections will continue to educate the public on the importance of City Hall. Whether this greater politicization of the electorate is exploited by the parties depends on the other factors.

Degree of Competition

As the structure of City Hall is opened up to more citizen participation through those reforming aldermen who have been elected, it should become progressively easier for the non-elected activists to crack City Hall's monopoly of expertise and obtain the information allowing them to become more effective in city politics. As the monopoly of the old guard is broken down, the parties will have more room to manoeuvre and establish their own base within the system.

Local Market

With the transformation of attitudes about urban problems and the greatly increased involvement of community groups in city politics, growing awareness of city issues should raise public acceptance of reform politics. The structural obstacles to party activity will remain, however, until legislative changes are made in the electoral process. A change in power or in policy at the provincial level could create a breakthrough in transforming the rules governing Toronto's municipal political market. Since the new municipal parties' provincial wings are in opposition this could only happen after the provincial election. Given a continuation of Conservative rule at Queen's Park the local market is unlikely to be reformed before the next municipal election in a way that will significantly ease the parties' electoral problems.

Product Differentiation

Without a democratization of the electoral rules it will be difficult for the parties to differentiate the product on ideological grounds, as the primary thrust will probably remain general urban reform. Any specific policy differences will continue to be obscured or distorted in the public's mind unless the media's ability to transmit issues dramatically improves. If the dominant group of "old guard" politicians were to be formalized as a party in self-defence, then the differentiation that is implicit could be made explicit to the public, enabling a more significant choice to be expressed through the election process. It is the politics of City Hall between elections that will be more decisive in achieving this polarization than the electoral campaign itself.

Consumer Sovereignty

To the extent that the voter-consumer is sovereign and that he is being educated by the increasing gravity of city problems to comprehend them in the three-dimensional perspective of local, provincial, and national relationships, one can expect the rate of abstention to decline and general public involvement by apartment dwellers and young people to rise. Whether the parties rather than independent candidates are able to gain from increasing voter turnout will depend on their success in simplifying the political choice and identifying across the city with common public concerns.

Strength of the Firm

The decisive factor will be the strength of the parties and their continuing determination to remain involved in municipal politics. This will turn on such non-municipal factors as the success of the parties at the federal and provincial levels, the views of the non-elected activists in the Toronto and District associations of the parties and their success or failure to enter municipal politics in other cities. The N.D.P's failure in Hamilton and other Ontario cities in 1970 municipal elections has reduced New Democrat enthusiasm for Toronto's next campaign.

Quality of the Product

The future of party politics in Toronto's municipal government will finally be determined by the parties' observed success or failure to respond to the changing needs of the urban political scene. In a transitional period with few representatives in City Hall the parties are having trouble maintaining their credibility as coherent political organizations. Given the wide ideological spectrum embraced by all parties at all levels of government, it will continue to be difficult for the new municipal wings to sharpen their political identity. Their long-term commitment to bring party politics to municipal government is likely to be challenged in the short term, before the rules of the electoral game are changed, by pressures to organize all the "progressive" candidates from all parties in a coalition to fight the "old guard."

A priori, one would expect any political system to offer resistance to fundamental transformations. Our review of the legal, psychological, and technological barriers to entry of parties into Toronto's city politics confirms this. But it also shows that, within the same geographical region, distinct political cultures can coexist at different constitutional levels, and that the public discriminates in its political behaviour between these levels of politics. More important, it reveals that the transmission of political change from one level of a political system to another is much more difficult than social scientists have generally assumed.

Analysis of any short stage of development must consider the long-term process. The Toronto experience suggests that, as in other cases of breaking out of restricting socio-political vicious circles, there may be increasing returns to efforts at change once certain breakthroughs have been made. Our micro-economist colleagues' theory of the firm does provide the examination of such a major case of systemic political change with an analytical framework. When we have several more years' experience in Toronto and other cities we may be in a position to develop an autonomous theory of party penetration more fully related to traditional concerns of comparative politics.

Central City Politics

HAROLD KAPLAN

While the cities that lie at the centres of our metropolitan areas are being faced with increasingly difficult problems, the record of city governments in dealing with these problems is unimpressive. It is true that city governments do not always get the necessary permission, financial assistance, and co-operation from higher levels of government. But in some cases the higher levels *do* provide money and encouragement, and yet very little – or nothing at all – happens. Putting all the blame for mounting traffic congestion, slums, and housing problems on the shoulders of the provincial government is a favourite device of local officials in evading their own responsibility. The fact is that very few city governments in Canada have launched a vigorous, comprehensive attack on the process of central-city decay.

The answer, I think, is that most city governments are *incapable* of such vigorous attacks, because political power at the local level is too dispersed. Political power in the average Canadian city government is broken up into little pieces and distributed among a variety of independent boards and commissions. Most mayors do not have the control over their own administrative officials that a provincial premier has over his officials. The absence of parties in Canadian city politics means that the mayor is not the effective leader of city government. Nor is any other city official able to provide leadership. Neither the mayor nor any other municipal official can formulate a program and assure the voters that he can carry out that

From *The Regional City* by Harold Kaplan (Toronto, Canadian Broadcasting Corporation, 1965), pp. 22-31.

program. No one in city government is in a position to pull together the various sub-centres of power. In short, the dispersive forces in Canadian city politics are far stronger than the forces of coordination and leadership.

The City of Toronto is a good illustration of the type of decentralized political system that prevails in Canadian cities today.

Toronto is governed by a twenty-three-member city council. The council consists of eighteen aldermen, two elected from each of nine wards in the city, and the mayor and four city controllers, who are elected at large. Like all large cities in Ontario, Toronto has a board of control, made up of the mayor and the city controllers. This board is collectively responsible for running the city administration. All administrative decisions, like hiring and firing or preparing the annual budget, are determined by a majority vote of the board. It also serves as the executive committee of the city council. All major actions of the council begin as recommendations of the board, and the aldermen, more often than not, go along with the board's proposals.

The mayor of Toronto is expected by the newspapers and civic groups to provide leadership. They strongly urge him to formulate a program and pilot it through council. But the mayor has no formal powers of his own, other than his one vote on the board of control. The mayor of Toronto usually formulates a program, but he is not in a position to carry it out.

On the surface this board of control plan might look like the cabinet system applied to city government. But the mayor's power over the board of control in no way approximates the prime minister's considerable power over his cabinet. The mayor, for example, has no control over the selection of the other board members; the four controllers are popularly elected and therefore feel no loyalty to the mayor. Moreover, all decisions on the board of control are made at public sessions and strictly by majority vote. The mayor's proposals often are defeated by the other controllers, and defeated in public for all to see.

In fact the pattern of politics in Toronto and other Ontario cities encourages controllers to reject the mayor's proposals. Most candidates for mayor are recruited from the board of control. When the mayor attends a board of control meeting, he is facing one or more of the men who will be running against him in the next election. It is as if Mr. Pearson's proposals had to be approved by a majority vote in a cabinet consisting of himself and Messrs. Diefenbaker, Douglas, Thompson, and Caouette. A controller interested in the mayor's job has a vested interest in defeating as many of the mayor's proposals as possible.

Finally, even where the mayor secures a majority on the board of control for one of his major proposals, that proposal can still be overturned by the full city council. The mayor has no political party to provide him with a consistent majority for his programs. He must construct temporary majorities for each of his proposals, in a council made up of twenty-three independent – and often unpredictable – individuals. In building a majority the mayor must rely on his lung power, on his ability to convince or shout down opponents of the proposals.

The trouble with this set-up is that the councillors are frequently ill-informed or indifferent to the major issues, and the resulting decisions are sometimes made in an off-hand manner. Or the councillors may find it easier to put off a decision indefinitely. Leadership is consistently frustrated.

Elections in Toronto are non-partisan, issueless and highly personal. Each candidate for city office runs and finances his own campaign. Candidates for council generally do not indicate whether they will support or oppose a particular mayor's program. If there is a race for mayor, the candidates for council will remain strictly neutral. No candidate for city office ever links his name to that of another candidate; there are no local alliances or blocs committed to pursuing a certain program in council. The candidates' campaigns are a combination of vague statements about "progress," along with specific promises about sidewalks and street lights. As a result, the voter is confronted with a long list of names – most of them unfamiliar – with no labels or civic parties to guide his choice.

In campaigning, each candidate places great reliance on his personal network of friends and acquaintances. A candidate will be strong in the neighbourhood where he lives or grew up, or where his wife grew up. Even candidates for a city-wide office, like controller or mayor, will base their campaigns on a few neighbourhoods where they have a large number of personal and business acquaintances.

The candidates emphasize their roots in a neighbourhood and

their willingness to service neighbourhood requests rather than the major issues facing the city. A candidate's length of residence in a neighbourhood and his ability to get sidewalks and street lights repaired will be stressed more heavily than the over-all problems of urban renewal, traffic, or public housing. A candidate's chances at the polls appear to depend largely on the familiarity of his name, his success in getting action on minor neighbourhood complaints, and his persistence in attending weddings, dances, picnics, and dinners.

As a result the city council of Toronto consists of people elected solely by their own efforts, and oriented more toward neighbourhood grievances than city-wide issues.

Leadership in this kind of non-partisan council is so arduous a task that some mayors have preferred to stress the social and ceremonial side of the office. They are content to preside over a caretaker administration, dealing only with a few critical problems that can't be ignored.

Another way in which power at the local level is decentralized, is by the delegation of major functions to independent boards and commissions. Public housing, town planning, and public health are usually vested in boards that are independent of the mayor and council on matters of policy and finance. The single most important and expensive municipal function, public education, is entrusted to an independent board of education.

The stated purpose of these independent boards is to protect certain governmental functions from something called "politics." Municipally owned enterprises like public housing or public transportation, it is argued, are run in a more business-like manner, if the politician's role in these operations is minimized. Some people claim that certain areas of public policy, like education, are too complex for a mayor and council to deal with adequately. Defenders of the independent boards equate the mayor and council with "politics," and claim that what the boards are doing is "non-political." Any attempt by a mayor to influence the city's educational policies is seen as political interference in the work of a non-political board.

In my view, these independent boards are clearly carrying out political, or policy-making, functions; and so why shouldn't these policies be made by politically responsible officials like the mayor and council? The independent commission device serves to shield policy decisions from public scrutiny, makes leadership in these areas difficult, and further weakens the effectiveness of the mayor. City government is a cumbersome machine, which any one individual – even if he is mayor – will find very difficult to move. If he fails to deliver on any of his campaign platform, it usually is not because of bad faith on his part.

This pattern is typical of many cities throughout Canada, where politics tends to be personal and unstructured, and where the organization of city government tends to be decentralized and sluggish.

There are two ways of providing more effective leadership at the local level. Cities in Great Britain and Western Europe have achieved some centralization of power through the use of party politics. There, the mayor, or whatever the chief executive is called, is strong because he can rely on stable majorities in council. A second solution, used in many American cities – sometimes in addition to local parties – is to strengthen the formal powers of the mayor. In these cities, the mayor is strong because he can hire and fire administrative personnel, prepare the budget, issue directives to administrative agencies, and even veto council decisions. In the European case the mayor is more like a prime minister; in the American case he is more like a president or governor.

Canadian city government borrows elements of both systems, but winds up with the worst of both worlds. The Canadian mayor is elected at large and expected to provide leadership, but he has neither a strong office nor a disciplined party behind him.

There are a few exceptions to this rule. Mayors in most British Columbia cities have more formal powers than the mayor of Toronto; but they still do not have as much power as an American strong-mayor. Moreover, cities like Edmonton, Vancouver, and Winnipeg *do* have local parties or factions in their civic elections. But these local parties, while running slates of candidates at election time, don't attempt to create disciplined party lines in the city council. The factional lines hold only during the election campaigns. Voting in the city council is usually just as personal and unpredictable in factional cities as in Toronto.

The only city with a disciplined local party is Montreal. Here, Mayor Jean Drapeau's Civic Party, which won a majority of the council seats in 1962, is clearly committed to a program, involving urban renewal, subway construction, and the amalgamation of all governments on the Island of Montreal. The Civic Party caucuses before each council meeting, agrees upon a course of action, and votes as a bloc at the regular council meetings. Only in Montreal has political power at the local level been pulled together. In fact, Montreal's ability to out-compete Toronto for the world's fair illustrates one advantage that a centralized political system has over a decentralized one.

Why do Canadians tolerate much weaker government at the city level than they would at the provincial or national level? The answer, in part, is that we don't take urban problems very seriously and are not greatly distressed at the failure of city governments to deal with these issues. We seem to feel that we can afford weak government at the local level more than we could afford it at the provincial or national level.

Furthermore, Canadian thinking about municipal government appears to have been heavily influenced by American ideas particularly by the American progressive movement of about sixty years ago. American progressives, like Teddy Roosevelt and Lincoln Steffens, were concerned about "bossism" and corrupt party machines dominating city government. They saw some decentralization of power as a protection against these corrupt machines. They disliked a strong-mayor system because the mayor often was a puppet of the party boss. The progressives also wanted more expertise and efficient administration in city government. The best way to achieve this goal, they thought, was to establish a commission of experts in a particular field of policy and then to give these experts administrative independence. This independence would protect them from politics, that is, from the mayor and the party boss. Finally, the progressives were convinced that parties in city politics inevitably meant inefficient and corrupt city government.

These American ideas have greatly influenced Canadian thinking about city government and the actual organization of Canadian city governments. In fact, the views of the progressives are far more influential in Canada today than in the United States. More recently there has been a reaction in the U.S. against the earlier notions, as seen in the reintroduction of parties or strong mayors into city politics. But nothing like that has occurred in Canada.

As a result of the American influence, there is a curious paradox in Canadian thinking about the various levels of government. The political ideas that Canadians accept in considering their federal and provincial governments – ideas largely derived from the British cabinet system – are rejected in considering the government of Canadian cities. In national politics Canadians believe that a focusing of power in the cabinet – and more specifically in the prime minister – permits the political leaders to get on with the job. Concentrated power also permits the voters to fix responsibility and to judge whether campaign platforms are being fulfilled. But at the local level a similar focusing of power in the hands of a mayor is viewed as opening the door to corruption and local dictators.

No one questions the House of Commons' right or ability to have the final say on questions of national defence or economic policy. But apparently the mayors and city councils cannot be trusted to decide questions of public education and public transportation. Political parties can be trusted to govern the nation but apparently can't be trusted to govern Winnipeg or Vancouver.

Even though parties would make the cumbersome machinery of city government operate more effectively, most Canadians staunchly defend the present pattern of non-partisan local politics. In most provinces, the major political parties have considered but rejected entrance into municipal politics, fearing that the voters would react against any party that intruded in the local sphere.

If provincial parties ran in city elections, we are told, the elections would be viewed as votes of confidence or no-confidence in the provincial cabinet, and would no longer focus on strictly local issues. But most of the important issues confronting the city are now regional, if not provincial, in scope. The *strictly* local issues, like garbage collection and sidewalk repair, are hardly worth being made the central issues in elections. In an age of increasing co-operation between levels of government, the idea of insulating local politics from provincial issues no longer makes sense.

It is also argued that parties would make municipal government more remote from the people. But this only means that a majority of the council would be committed to a program and would be less swayed by the pressures of the moment. Ratepayers' associations, newspapers, and other local groups might find a partisan council less intimidated by their noisy protests and thus more remote. And others mean by "remote" that partisan local elections would end the present, highly personal style of campaigning, built around friends, neighbours, and business associates.

Another defence of the present system is that there are no issues in municipal government over which parties can differ, that local government is simply a matter of efficient or inefficient administration. But, in my view, there do not appear to be any issues at the local level only because non-partisan politics submerges them. Partisan elections do not always emphasize and clarify the important issues of the day but they do so more often than personalized, non-partisan elections do.

The prevalence of honest and efficient partisan governments in the cities of Great Britain and Western Europe should lay most Canadian fears about local parties to rest. And many may be disappointed to hear that there is very little corruption and there are very few bosses left in American city government. Nor are there any major differences, on this score, between partisan and non-partisan American cities. Canadian fears about local parties, using American cities as prime illustrations, are based largely on the way American cities looked in 1900, at the time of the progressive movement.

But I do concede two major shortcomings in the idea of partisan local government. Most American and British cities that have partisan elections are dominated by one party – the Democrats in the U.S. and Labour in Britain. Many of these cities lack any intelligent criticism of policies pursued by the majority party. The other shortcoming is that a Canadian city run by the Liberals, let us say, probably would have badly strained relations with a Tory provincial government; and no city can afford to quarrel with its mother province. This difficulty could be avoided if cities developed purely local parties, which had no relation – friendly or otherwise – to the provincial parties. But this idea of an autonomous local party system, while good in theory, is almost never attained in practice.

In addition to public attitudes there are also political motives behind the continuation of decentralized government at the city level. Provincial governments find it easier to get their way in bargaining with weakly integrated city governments. The provincial officials also find it easier to influence the decisions of particular local agencies, if these agencies are independent of the mayor and council.

The head of the provincial party in power, moreover, may fear that a strong mayor in a city like Toronto, Montreal, or Winnipeg would be a threat to his leadership of the province. Such a mayor would appoint as many administrative officials and control as large a budget as the premier himself. Whether in the opposition or the ruling party, the strong mayor would pose a threat to the premier's job.

Finally, this decentralization of power persists because many local officials show no strong desire to centralize powers. When given an opportunity to abolish some independent agency, like a transit commission, and assume the power directly, city councils often vote against a take-over. Many local officials like having the difficult decisions made elsewhere. Then these officials can join the ratepayers' associations in denouncing the independent agency for its high-handed behaviour.

One final explanation of inactivity at the local level has less to do with the structure of city government and elections, and more to do with the people who run the cities. It is my unpleasant duty to report that the level of talent among elected officials in municipal government is low. Provincial and national affairs appear to drain off most of the talent in politics today. Although there are some conspicuous exceptions, local politicians often seem incapable of visualizing the city's problems or understanding the proposed solutions. Often the key difference among city politicians is not between two points of view on a major issue, but between those who have any point of view and those who have none. The major problems facing the city are not met partly because the ideas of many local politicians do not go beyond repairing street lights and putting more benches at bus stops.

There is no easy solution to the problem of attracting more talent into local politics; but I think we might begin by making local, elected office more significant and attractive. We should consider lengthening the term of mayor and councillors to four years, decreasing the size of councils, making the job of councillor a full-time one carrying a full-time salary, and shifting more power from independent boards or commissions to the mayor and council. Parties, I think, would help raise the level of local political personnel, by actively recruiting talented people and by relieving candidates of the necessity to finance their own campaigns.

Now that our cities are faced with staggering problems in the fields of welfare and urban renewal, they badly need more capable political leaders and leaders who are in a political position to carry out proposed solutions. My proposed reforms involve nothing more radical than the application of centralized responsibility and party politics now practised at the provincial and federal levels to city government.

The Rise of Party Politics in Canadian Local Elections

JAMES LIGHTBODY

Recent changes in the political face of Metropolitan Toronto have become apparent with the open involvement of the Liberal and New Democratic Party machines in the pursuit of municipal office. This intervention into the nominally nonpartisan elections of one of Canada's larger urban centres apparently has provoked considerable anguish for some knowledgeable students of Canadian politics, suggesting that we are due an appraisal of the role of these national parties in the evolving Canadian urban context.

Part of the problem in coming to grips with this open party involvement stems from the conscious desire to view municipal government as existing apart from the political competition at senior levels of government. This attitude is reminiscent of the variety of municipal reform movements, clean government and nonpartisanship leagues so active in American local politics during the early part of this century. In the United States these associations found their genesis as a logical response to the patronage-dependent, boss-dominated pattern of their contemporary local institutions. A generation of American social leadership was obsessed with the morality plays which legitimated the insulation of local governing bodies from the less than fanciful whims of the bosses. That the myth of nonpartisanship and the reality of urban political organization were to become incongruent (as witness the *nonpartisan* city regime of Mayor Richard Daley in Chicago) demonstrates clearly the continuing need for informal mechanisms beyond the larger urban governmental structures which are able to translate the expectations, wants

From: *Journal of Canadian Studies*, Vol. 6, (February, 1971), pp. 39-44. Reprinted by permission.

and demands of citizens into official policy decisions. The most effective and responsive of these mechanisms can be established political parties.

Despite the fact that embryo Canadian municipal reform movements have both employed the rhetoric of their American cousins and embraced institutional reforms developed to meet American political circumstances (for one example, in the introduction to Canada of the city manager style of administration), this response to the Canadian local political environment may not be appropriate. Perhaps a more reliable model on which to pattern our behaviour is to be found in British political experience. As our urbanizing system evolves toward the complex relationships of urban metropolitan organization, it will become increasingly necessary to develop more open and responsive instrumentalities to secure coherent civic administration. The traditionally élite-dominated, nonpartisan, clean government movements have not proven able to adapt quickly enough.

The rapid urbanization of the Canadian political system since World War II has produced significant changes in popular expectations of the great role which local government is to assume in its traditional functions of social development, the provision of primary services and, most recently, environmental control. If this tier of Canadian government is not expected to develop as the mere administrative agency for provincial, and in some instances, federal officials in the implementation of policy derived through their own political channels, then its claims to an independent realm of political authority must quickly be proven viable and legitimate.

A good part of the current difficulty in the appreciation of partisanship as a convenient mechanism for organization in the conduct of municipal affairs results from uncritical acceptance of American experience and rationalization of our activities in these terms. The preoccupation of American social science until recently with quantifiable knowledge of consensus politics, the dilution of socio-political conflict and the academic construction of models of stable democratic systems led to analyses of urban political communities which emphasized the distribution of power among élite and non-élite societal groups. For Canadian purposes this suggested at best the reform of existing mechanisms to facilitate the integration of less powerful groups into the decision-making process. This orientation could not kindly countenance an approach to urban politics contradictory to American experience, emphasizing political conflict through partisan alignment as a means of influencing and gaining power over profoundly political decisions. It is not surprising that the primary corrective of current abuses in the American circumstance, prescribed by their contemporary social engineers, asserts a return to issue-oriented social action groups as the basic mechanism for political action. This trend, as noted below, has also found its way to Canada.

It may, indeed, be possible to introduce governmental institutions into communities to which they are not indigenous, but it is quite another question to transfer the informal administrative accords, legal traditions and political organization which make viable the constitutional arrangements. Unique factors in the Canadian environment, both social and institutional, have produced a political system rather different from that of either the United States or Great Britain. While it is not surprising that our resulting process is not entirely native but largely derived from the experience of these systems, perhaps we do find ourselves at present ill-equipped with the concepts appropriate to relevant political activity.

There exists, however, some evidence that the apolitical nature of Canadian municipal politics has evolved in response to factors peculiar to the Canadian political environment. First, and most directly analogous to the American experience, has been the pattern of western expansion and rural, agrarian domination of our political process. Frontier existence and the rural life-style is one which emphasizes community co-operation, apparent not only in the network of local economic institutions but in political life as well. The anti-party ideology which flavoured the early period of the western Canadian protest movement was a northern extension of American agrarian populism. But the logical expectation of community co-operation in the development of elementary services in a rugged natural environment was clearly self-evident and not a matter open to political debate (hence roads, schools and the provisions of justice became the first functions of local government). The small population base for most communities reinforced a social homogeneity already provided by preoccupation with a common enemy in nature, and reduced substantially the prospect of lasting socio-economic cleavage as a source for political division.

While this approach to politics was critically necessary to the survival of the original frontier communities, the continuing Canadian fascination with the land, the unoccupied northern frontier and the agrarian basis of our society, has concurrently maintained the façade of co-operative rural communities. This, in turn, has fostered an acceptance of local nonpartisanship as a prerequisite to legitimate politics. This tendency has had the unfortunate consequence of disguising both the true urban nature of our society and the very real sources of political cleavage induced by this type of complex social system. The expression of these divisions, when eventually exerted through political parties representative of them, appears at more distant governmental levels, manifestly less competent in their resolution.

Second, it can be argued that the local political process developed roots independent of party for the simple reason that there existed slight need in Canada for an efficient precinct and ward level party organization. In the United States the prerequisite of voter registration in advance of elections fought at regular and predictable intervals, with nomination often through the political primary process, encouraged intensive organized political activity. In Britain, the early development of the Labour Party as a vehicle requiring the mass organization and political action of a social class, forced local electoral participation on to the party as a means of maintaining the continual mobilization of party activists for the always pending possibility of a general election. The growing tendency of British pundits to view local electoral results as barometric readings of national political opinion has not diminished the stakes for national parties in producing results at the local level. Moreover, power held through offices at the borough level provides an organizational base for a party in opposition at Westminster, in much the same way as Canadian political parties seek provincial surrogates to power in Ottawa.

The absence of an effective municipal party system in Canada can generally be traced to the absence of these, or parallel, critical factors in our political development. Thus since Canadian politics has not been graced with an intensively mobilized mass working-class party, dependent for success on the disciplined turnout of its membership, we have not seen this careful national political cultivation of urban areas. Since Canadian electoral arrangements, moreover, do not encourage party activity in the education, registration and primary participation of the urban voter in the same fashion as in the United States, this incentive to partisan politicization of the cities is also lacking. The federal structure of Canadian institutions, including the national political parties, places greater rewards on the capture of provincial power than municipal. In all instances, then, little reason exists for political parties to expend even a slight part of their limited resources in Canadian municipal politics.

This suggests a third factor in the apoliticism of civic politics. One of the least disputed of the delegations of power under the Canadian constitution makes municipal governments creatures of provincial legislatures. This provision has two consequences. First, civic administrations are legitimate institutions only in their position as subordinate adjuncts of the province. Second, as soon as the normal administration of traditionally municipal functions becomes too great a problem for local government to manage, usually due to the financial burden on the limited municipal property tax base, the provincial legislature normally exercises its authority by relieving municipalities of these responsibilities.[1] The stakes of the game lie in the control of the Legislative Assembly.

Because of the lack of significant independent authority, the sandbox politics of City Hall offer little incentive for organized partisan activity or division. By demonstrated reality the cities appear more vulnerable to pressure by special groups, most usually real estate and construction interests, whose livelihood *is* affected by decisions within the limited jurisdiction of municipal councils (for example, zoning by-laws). Given the Canadian geography of urban development with but one or two large urban centres in each province, it is quite likely that provincial administrations will maintain their reluctance to delegate sufficient power to the cities to permit them to compete as equals for public attention or to develop as countervailing power centres to the provincial regimes. Political parties evolve to exercise influence in the decision-taking processes of a community: when the power to take significant decisions is lacking, it is not surprising that organized parties are not involved in the process.

By way of contrast, the complicated constitutional arrangements

[1] Thus, for example, the extraordinary expense incurred in the provision of educational services has occasioned most provinces to expand their administrative intervention in proportion to the direct amount of provincial financial assistance.

in most American states provide local institutions with home-rule authority, an autonomous field for political action which effectively restricts the state government's natural inclination to intervene. Progressive reformers, by attempting to sterilize the politics of urban areas through the widespread proliferation of non-political, often elective, independent boards, agencies and commissions for the administrative supervision of various local government functions, in effect further strengthened the latent demand for a level of para-institutional politics to co-ordinate these activities. Given both a legislative arena in which to operate and the classic function of parties in the co-ordinated aggregation and expression of demands upon it, the re-emergence of party organizations in the larger American cities even after the progressive reforms should not have been unanticipated. While political parties are certainly not the sole means of achieving recognition of interest, they are nonetheless an important mechanism for the traditional functions of filling elective positions, activating electors and providing a minimum level of literacy about contentious issues. The greater the complexity of the political community, the more important this type of formalized association becomes.

The historically nonpartisan nature of Canadian municipal elections has appeared then as a result of the early agrarian frontier pattern of development (and the nostalgia of its continued mythology), the lack of pressure from the larger system for efficient urban party organization, and the slight scope for autonomous decision-making assigned to local municipalities. If these factors are not still relevant, then there is reason to argue that competitive municipal elections fought among partisans of nationally organized parties are not a current aberration but are likely to form a new pattern in Canadian urban politics.

It is most obvious that Canada is no longer a rural society. Well over three-quarters of our population can be classified as urban and by 1980 over sixty per cent will live and work in a score of our major metropolitan areas. Any intensively urban, industrial society such as Canada's has become is comprised of a complex network of social interaction, becoming a fragile, co-operative and tightly interdependent system whose viability is absolutely contingent upon the continuing adaptation of social and political instruments to newly generated needs for regulation. The assumption by individuals of particular roles in this new urban community, and their subsequent assignment as classes to social positions begins the process of group self-awareness. The appearance of group identity underlies the articulation of the group's interest, the generation of political division on this basis and the eventual extinction of non-party politics at the municipal level.

In Canada socialist candidates and parties have for some time been a fixture in local government elections, but the rapid urbanization of the post-war period generated a growing "blue-collar" consciousness and forced the New Democratic Party, in its self-assumed stance as the Canadian working-class party, to make a heavy commitment to solidifying this basis of its support. Official N.D.P. candidates have begun to appear with increasing regularity in the local council elections of our major English-speaking cities. Actually, political partisans under a number of *ad hoc* associational guises have intervened in the electoral battles of our larger cities, most notably Montreal, Toronto, Winnipeg and Vancouver in the past. With only a small cadre of upper middle class activists at their disposal, these action groups have emphasized their own progressive bias while quietly masking their real aim in preventing the socialists from gaining control over the city coffers. Although willing to devote considerable debate to the analysis of detail, these groups are rarely able to enforce voting discipline sufficient to co-ordinate the executive activities of municipal administration with any continuity.

The most singular exception to this approach has been Jean Drapeau's Civic Party in Montreal. The party achieved power originally on the strength of an appeal for civic morality, the personal character of Jean Drapeau and, most importantly, the support of key leadership groups in metropolitan Quebec society who had been alienated from the Duplessis regime. It is not improbable that Drapeau's own success will end as many of these same groups affiliate with the leadership of the Parti Québecois and its civic organizational "front" (FRAP) in an appeal for working-class support in municipal elections.

Despite the occasional foray, party loyalists have not, until recently, extended the scope of their involvement into a full assault on municipal office. The change in attitude results from the increase in the spoils at stake. There are a number of reasons for this change of heart. In the first place, the electoral redistribution preceding the

1968 federal general election, by according the majority urban population an appropriate share of the ridings, has emphatically alerted the politically aware to the impact of the metropolitan vote in the shaping of future federal and provincial governments. A more equitable provincial redistribution in Manitoba, for example, was to a very large extent an ally of the N.D.P. in its 1969 victory. Coupled with this has been the emergence of the N.D.P. as a mass, urban and predominantly working-class party, to whose electoral advantage a fairer distribution of the urban ridings has worked. Both as a result of and in order to maintain the usually higher intensity in the commitment of its adherents, and to retain its organizational effectiveness between elections, the N.D.P. has quite naturally made the leap to open municipal involvement. If other national parties are not to be outflanked in the organization of the core metropolitan areas, the necessary response has to be an electoral challenge.

Thirdly, there is little question that the problems of urban local government have grown both more apparent and more acute in the immediate past. City planning, environmental control, housing, transportation, and community development are problems which grow geometrically with the expansion of urban areas, and which at the same time are functions not easily assumed by provincial governments. Grudging acceptance by the provinces of the necessity for a realm of municipal activity has been accentuated by a trend toward regional and metropolitan units of government, in short a rationalization of existing political institutions towards larger and more financially viable local communities. The net result of these factors has appeared in the professionalization of local government politics. Elected officials are required to specialize to deal with complicated detail, to expand proportionately their investment of time in the management of local affairs, and to compete for re-election against increasingly articulate, politically aware persons who have become involved as the new possibilities for effective decision-taking have appeared.

There is surely a factor of community size to be considered here. Beyond a certain critical point, likely in the neighbourhood of three or four thousand persons, the scope of the functions to be performed by a local government, coupled with the probable lack of social homogeneity in cities of this size, provide a basis and a need for co-ordinated political action. The satisfactory governing of the locality can no longer be supplied by a handful of community notables with an independent sense of *noblesse oblige*: the process of professionalizing local politics is begun and with it is established the need for an organized party system.

Even given these arguments that suggest reasons for the growing involvement of established political parties in local government elections, it is by no means inevitable that parties will be the *exclusive* mechanism by which city politics of the future are shaped. Indeed the recent impressive growth of issue-oriented pressure groups has led more than one commentator to suggest that parties themselves are in a relative state of decline at even the federal level. If one thing does appear certain, however, it is that parties will become much more deeply wedded to the civic politics of Canada's larger metropolitan centres. I have considered a number of reasons for the apparent existence of this trend, but is this national party involvement to be encouraged? The most substantial arguments advanced in support of this intervention relate to the contributions parties are likely to make in facilitating responsible control of community administration and, secondly, in the potential for policy innovation which they are able to introduce into the city's government.

In the first place, a major part of the provincial government's distrust of local politicians has been based on the suspicion that they are neither very representative nor can they be held effectively responsible by electors for services under their administration. By placing multiple, supervisory checks on local government decisions, and through statutory delegation of particular functions to roughly autonomous boards and commissions (for example in the independent authority given school boards or utilities commissions), the province further diminishes rather than expands the potential for responsible government. Of course, the introduction of partisanship to local councils will not directly affect the formal distribution of responsibilities: this provincial prerogative will be exercised only as pressure is brought on Cabinet. What is likely to occur in the larger metropolitan areas following the routinization of the municipal party system is the gradual return of functions to local council control as parties, finding themselves subjected to a rigorous competition for office, expand their programs in the form of pressure on the province to maximize their responsibilities for all local services. The effective collective responsibility of a local government "ministry" with authority over the spectrum of civic services should theoretically facilitate both more satisfactory and fiscally efficient local administration, and better control by the electorate of a clearly visible governmental group that can be held accountable for their activities.

Much of the confusion and apathy that are the trademarks of local government politics in Canada are a direct consequence of the inability of the local citizenry to fix responsibility on either an institution (is it a school board, water district, public utilities commission or town council decision with which one is at odds?) or a given group of persons on such a body. The traditional notion in local government circles of the individual responsibility of each of the aldermen may be acceptable on the tiny scale of rural municipalities or of smaller towns and cities where they and their activities are well known. But in the complex government of the greater metropolitan areas of Canada it is apparent that a style of collective responsibility is necessary for co-ordination in the implementation of policy and subsequently in the accountability of those responsible for that policy. Here again the Civic Party of Mayor Drapeau provides an instructive example of the dynamic effects of tightly-knit party organization in the executive direction of municipal government.

Finally, we must consider the question of policy initiation in the civic political process. Confined by the characteristics of their roles, city councillors can rarely be creative or innovative in general public policy terms. By lack of innovative capacity, I mean that a council is unable to perceive dramatic change in the life style of its political community. Even if acknowledged, the council is institutionally inhibited in producing the radical departures in policy needed to cope with the new demands expressed by residents. As an aggregation of independents lacking informal mechanisms for organized action, the council is forced to seek consensus in precedent whenever a genuine policy conflict develops. Generally, the social bias of most councils favours a conservative orientation toward restriction of governmental services to maintain the lowest possible level of taxation on the property base. This is to be expected in those largely suburban and rural communities in which the electorate is extensively property-owning. But in the larger urban core areas, the demands on local government are for a significant change in the approach to urban living, in essence for a broader initiative on the part of the city council. The fears of established aldermen (and the interests they represent) of what this will mean fiscally and politically is reflected in the recent abortive attempt of Toronto city council to gerrymander ward boundaries to the serious disadvantage of downtown residents.

While it is true that the institutional structure of Canadian metropolitan governments in Toronto, Winnipeg, and most recently Montreal, has been adapted with greater direction and success than is possible in the United States, it is also the case that it has been provincial governments with their strong legislative authority which have produced the change. If Canadian provincial governments had been as weakened by the traditional hostility between executive and legislature as have been the American states, then it could be argued that the pattern of self-interested municipal wrangling, which has effectively restricted institutional innovation in the United States, would have emerged pre-eminent in Canada as well.

All this suggests that the larger metropolitan units will require the type of organized political control which parties can provide if they are able to convert the wants of their electorates into policy and administer it effectively. The need for this organization in council decision-making will become more obvious as issue-oriented action groups grow increasingly professional in the expression of demands before local councils. The fragmentation of municipal councils as aldermen seek sanctuary when faced with the prospect of reaching personal decisions in response to the spokesmen for these public demands will decline only as party discipline intervenes. Parties will necessarily appear not only to reduce these demands to coherent policies, but also to retain the allegiance of the urban policy's active leadership cadre through successful co-option into the greater political party system.

In sum, it is my expectation that parties will adapt and respond to the complex challenges of our urban political communities. Under appropriate leadership they may become effective instruments for the reassertion of community control over government administration and for the generation of a public policy responsive to the demands of articulate civic leaders.

Bibliography

Canadian

Alexander, Alan, "The Institutional and Role Perceptions of Local Aldermen," paper presented at the annual meeting of the Canadian Political Science Association, Winnipeg, June 4, 1970.

Bourassa, Guy, "Les Elites Politiques de Montreal: De L'Aristrocratie a la democratie," *Canadian Journal of Economics and Political Science*, 31 (February, 1965), pp. 35-51.

Brittain, H. L., *Local Government in Canada* (Toronto: Ryerson Press, 1951).

Burdeyny, Bill, "Party Politics and Regional Government," *The Future City: A Selection of Views on the Reorganization of Government in Greater Winnipeg*, ed., Lloyd Axworthy (Winnipeg: The Institute of Urban Studies, University of Winnipeg 1971), pp. 34-38.

Bureau of Municipal Research, "Good Candidates Make Good Elections," *Civic Affairs Bulletin* (Toronto: November, 1959).

______, "The Metro Politician – A Profile," *Civic Affairs Bulletin* (Toronto: June, 1963).

Clarkson, Stephen, "Barriers to Entry of Parties into Toronto's Civic Politics: Towards a Theory of Party Penetration," *Canadian Journal of Political Science*, 4 (June, 1971), pp. 206-223.

Crawford, Kenneth G., *Canadian Municipal Government* (Toronto: University of Toronto Press, 1954).

Donnelly, M. S., "Ethnic Participation in Municipal Government: Winnipeg, St. Boniface and the Metropolitan Corporation of Greater Winnipeg," *Politics and Government of Urban Canada*, eds., Lionel D. Felman and M. D. Goldrick (Toronto: Methuen, 1969), pp. 61-71.

Easton, Robert, and Tennant, Paul, "Vancouver Civic Party Leadership: Backgrounds, Attitudes, and Non-civic Party Affiliations," *B. C. Studies*, 2 (Summer, 1969), pp 9-26.

Feldman, Lionel D., and Goldrick, Michael D., eds., *Politics and Government of Urban Canada* (Toronto: Methuen, 1969).

Fowler, E. P., and Goldrick, M.D., "Patterns of Partisan and Non-Partisan Balloting," *Parties to Change: The Introduction of Political Parties in the 1969 Toronto Municipal Election* (Toronto: Bureau of Municipal Research, 1971), pp. 34-45.

Gaetz, H. H., "Government a Question of Business," *Public Service Magazine*, 6 (June, 1909), pp. 177-179.

"Municipal Legislation," *The Western Municipal News*, 4 (March, 1909), pp. 1078-1081.

Granatstein, J. L., "The New City Politics," *The Canadian Forum*, (January, 1970), p. 226.

———, [Reply to Stephen Clarkson] *The Canadian Forum*, (March, 1970), p. 288.

Hough, Jerry F., "Voters' Turnout and the Responsiveness of Local Government: The Case of Toronto," *Politics: Canada*, ed., Paul W. Fox (Toronto: McGraw-Hill, 1970), pp. 284-299.

Joyce, John G., and Hosse, H. A., *Civic Parties in Canada* (Montreal: Canadian Federation of Mayors and Municipalities, 1970).

Kamin, Leon J., "Ethnic and Party Affiliations of Candidates as Determinants of Voting," *Canadian Journal of Psychology*, 12 (December, 1958), pp. 205-212.

Kaplan, Harold, "Politics and Policy-Making in Metropolitan Toronto," *Canadian Journal of Political Science*, 31 (November, 1965), pp. 538-551.

———, *The Regional City: Politics and Planning in Metropolitan Areas* (Toronto: Canadian Broadcasting Corporation, 1965).

———, *Urban Political Systems: A. Functional Analysis of Metro Toronto* (New York: Columbia University Press, 1967).

Lightbody, James, "The Rise of Party Politics in Canadian Local Elections," *Journal of Canadian Studies*, 6 (February, 1971), pp. 39-44.

Lighthall, W. D., "The Elimination of Political Parties in Canadian Cities," *National Municipal Review*, 6 (March, 1917), pp. 207-209.

Lorimer, James, *The Real World of City Politics* (Toronto: James Lewis and Samuel, 1970).

Michaelson, Peter, "Montreal's Civic Party: the King, the Duke and the Vassals," *Civic Administration*, 19 (April, 1968), pp. 38, 39, 56.

Morgan, Frank, "The New Order: Purpose, Discipline at City Hall," *Civic Administration*, 20 (June, 1968), pp. 29-32.

Munro, William Bennet, *American Influences on Canadian Government* (Toronto: The Macmillan Company of Canada Ltd., 1929).

Phillips, A., "Modern Manual of Graft in Civic Office; Corruption," *Maclean's Magazine*, 75 (March, 1963), pp. 36-43.

Plunkett, Thomas J., *Urban Canada and Its Government: A Study of Municipal Organization* (Toronto: The Macmillan Company of Canada Ltd., 1968).

Rowat, Donald C., *Your Local Government* (Toronto: The Macmillan Company of Canada Ltd., 1962).

______, *The Canadian Municipal System: Essays on the Improvement of Local Government* (Toronto: McClelland and Stewart Ltd., 1969).

Sharpe, J. W., "Government by Commission," *Municipal World*, 22 (December, 1912), pp. 273-276.

Short., "Municipal Government by Commission," *Canadian Municipal Journal*, 3 (April, 1907), pp. 143-146.

Silcox, Peter, "Everybody's Urban Crisis," *The Canadian Forum* (May, 1969), pp. 36-37.

______, "Postscript: the City Council Results," *Parties to Change: the Introduction of Political Parties in the 1969 Toronto Municipal Election* (Toronto: Bureau of Municipal Research, 1971), pp. 5-13.

______, "The Beginning of Change," *Parties to Change: the Introduction of Political Parties in the 1969 Toronto Municipal Election* (Toronto: Bureau of Municipal Research, 1971), pp. 5-13.

Wickett, Samuel Morley., *City Government in Canada* (Toronto: University of Toronto Library, 1902).

Young, W. D., "We Need Party Politics in Civic Government," *Maclean's Magazine*, 72 (September, 1959), pp. 10, 53, 54.

American

Adrian, Charles R., "A Typology of Nonpartisan Elections," *Western Political Quarterly*, 12 (June, 1959), pp. 449-458.

______, "Some General Characteristics of Non-Partisan Elections," *American Political Science Review*, 56 (September, 1952), pp. 766-776.

Adrian, Charles R., and Press, Charles, *Governing Urban America* (New York: McGraw Hill, third edition 1968).

Alford, Robert R., and Scoble, Harry M., "Sources of Local Political Involvement," *American Political Science Review*, 62 (December, 1968), pp. 1192-1206.

Alford, Robert R., and Lee, Eugene C., "Voting Turnout in American Cities," *American Political Science Review*, 62 (September, 1968), pp. 796-813.

Banfield, Edward C., and Wilson, James Q., *City Politics* (Cambridge: Harvard University Press, 1963).

Bosworth, Karl., "The Manager Is a Politician," *Public Administration Review*, 18 (Summer, 1958), pp. 216-222.

Bromage, Arthur W., "Partisan Elections in Cities," *National Municipal Review*, 40 (May, 1951), pp. 250-253.

Conway, Margaret M., "Political Participation in a Nonpartisan Local Election," *Public Opinion Quarterly*, 32 (Fall, 1969), pp. 425-430.

______, "Voter Information Sources in a Nonpartisan Local Election," *Western Political Quarterly*, 71 (March, 1968), pp. 69-77.

Cushman, Robert E., "Nonpartisan Nominations and Elections," *The Annals of the American Academy of Political and Social Sciences*, 106 (March, 1923), pp. 83-96.

Cutright, Phillips, "Nonpartisan Electoral Systems in American Cities," *Comparative Studies in Society and History*, 5 (January, 1963), pp. 212-226.

Ellis, Ellen D., "National Parties and Local Politics," *American Political Science Review*, 29 (February, 1935), pp. 60-67.

Eulau, Heinz, Zink, Betty H., and Prewitt, Kenneth, "Latent Partisanship in Nonpartisan Elections: Effects of Political Milieu and Mobilization," *The Electoral Process*, eds., M. K. Jennings and L. H. Zeigler (Englewood Cliffs, New Jersey: Prentice-Hall, 1966), pp. 208-237.

Freeman, J. L., "Local Party Systems: Theoretical Considerations and a Case Analysis," *American Journal of Sociology*, 64 (November, 1958), pp. 282-289.

Gilbert, Charles, and Clague, Christopher, "Electoral Competition and Electoral Systems in Large Cities," *Journal of Politics*, 24 (May, 1962), pp. 323-349.

Gilbert, Charles, "Some Aspects of Nonpartisan Elections in Large Cities," *Midwest Journal of Political Science*, 6 (1962), pp. 345-362.

Gosnell, Harold F., *Machine Politics: Chicago Style* (Chicago: Chicago University Press, 1937).

Greenstein, Fred. I., "The Changing Pattern of Urban Party Politics," *The Annals of the American Academy of Political and Social Science*, 353 (May, 1964), pp. 1-13.

Hagensick, A., "Influences of Partisanship and Incumbency on a Nonpartisan Election System," *Western Political Quarterly*, 17 (March, 1964), pp. 117-124.

Hawkins, Brett W., "A Note on Urban Political Structure, Environment and Political Integration," *Polity*, 2 (Fall, 1969), pp. 32-48.

Herson, Lawrence., "The Lost World of Municipal Government," *American Political Science Review*, 51 (June, 1957), pp. 330-345.

Kessel, John H., "Governmental Structure and Political Environment: A Statistical Note About American Cities," *American Political Science Review*, 56 (September, 1962), pp. 615-620.

Lee, Eugene C., *The Politics of Nonpartisanship* (Berkeley: University of California Press, 1960).

Lineberry, Robert L., and Fowler, Edmund P., "Reformism and Public Policies in American Cities," *American Political Science Review*, 61 (September, 1967), pp. 701-716.

Mayo, Charles G., "The 1961 Mayoralty Election in Los Angeles: The Political Party in a Nonpartisan Election," *Western Political Quarterly*, 17 (June, 1964), pp. 325-339.

Orleans, Peter, "Urban Politics and the Nonpartisan Ballot: A Metropolitan Case," *The New Urbanization*, eds., Scott Greer *et al.* (New York: St. Martin's Press, 1968), pp. 287-298.

Pomper, G. "Ethnic and Group Voting in Non-Partisan Municipal Elections," *Public Opinion Quarterly*, 30 (Spring, 1966), pp. 79-97.

Riordon, William L., *Plunkett of Tammany Hall* (New York: E. D. Dutton and Co., 1963).

Salisbury, Robert, and Black, Gordon, "Class and Party in Partisan and Nonpartisan Elections: The Case of Des Moines," *American Political Science Review*, 58 (September, 1963), pp. 584-592.

Salisbury, Robert, "St. Louis Politics: Relationships Among Interests, Parties, and Governmental Structure," *Western Political Quarterly*, 13 (June, 1960), pp. 498-507.

Schnore, Leo F., and Alford, Robert, "Forms of Government and Socio-Economic Characteristics of Suburbs," *Administrative Science Quarterly*, 8 (June, 1963), pp. 1-17.

Sherbenou, E. L., "Class, Participation, and the Council-Manager Plan," *Public Administration Review*, 21 (Summer, 1961), pp. 13-35.

Stewart, Frank, *A Half Century of Municipal Reform: The History of the National Municipal League* (Berkeley: University of California Press, 1950).

Williams, Oliver P., and Adrian, Charles R., *Four Cities: A Study in Comparative Policy-Making* (Philadelphia: University of Pennsylvania Press, 1963).

______, "The Insulation of Local Politics under the Nonpartisan Ballot," *American Political Science Review*, 53 (December, 1959), pp. 1052-1063.

Wilson, James Q., and Banfield, Edward C., "Public Regardingness as a Value Premise in Voting Behavior," *American Political Science Review*, 58 (December, 1964), pp. 876-887.

Wolfinger, Raymond E., and Field, J., "Political Ethos and the Structure of City Government," *American Political Science Review*, 60 (June, 1966), pp. 306-326.

Wolfinger, Raymond E. "The Development and Persistence of Ethnic Voting," *American Political Science Review*, 59 (December, 1965), pp. 896-906.

British

Bechel, J. M., "The Recruitment of Local Councillors: A Case Study," *Political Studies*, 14 (1966), pp. 360-364.

Birch, A. H. *Small Town Politics: A Study of the Political Life in Glossop* (London: Oxford University Press, 1969).

Blondel, J., and Hall, R., "Conflict, Decision-Making and the Perception of Local Councillors," *Political Studies*, 15 (October, 1967), pp. 322-350.

Brenan, T., Conney, E. W., and Pollins H., "Party Politics and Local Government in Western South Wales," *Political Quarterly*, 25 (1954), pp. 76-83.

Budge, I., "Electors Attitudes to Local Government: A Survey of a Glasgow Constituency," *Political Studies*, 13 (1965), pp. 386-392.

Bulpitt, J. G., *Party Politics in English Local Government* (London: Longmans, 1967).

Fletcher, Peter, "An Explanation of Variations in 'Turnout' in Local Elections," *Political Studies*, 17 (December, 1969), pp. 495-502.

Keith-Lucas, Bryan, "Party Politics in English Local Government," *Queen's Quarterly*, 68 (Autumn, 1961), pp. 467-472.

Lee, J. M., *Social Leaders and Public Persons* (London: Oxford University Press, 1963).

MacColl, James E., "The Party System in English Local Government," *Public Administration*, 27 (1949), pp. 69-75.

Sharp, L. J., *Voting in Cities: the 1964 Borough Elections* (London: Macmillan, 1967).

Warren, J. H., "The Party System in Local Government," *The British Party System*, ed., Sydney Bailey (London: Hansard Society, 1952), pp. 177-192.

Index